# President Clinton
# and the Working Man

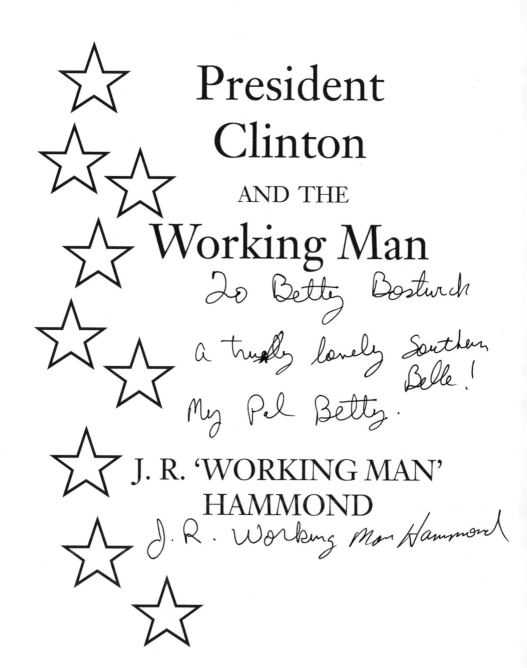

# President Clinton

# Clinton

## AND THE

# Working Man

*To Betty Bostwick*

*a truely lovely Southern Belle !*

*My Pal Betty.*

## J. R. 'WORKING MAN' HAMMOND

*J. R. Working Man Hammond*

BLACK BELT PRESS
Montgomery

BLACK BELT PRESS
P.O. Box 551
Montgomery, AL 36101

ISBN 1-881320-32-4

5993 Old Huntsville Rd.
McCalla, Al
35711

Library of Congress Cataloging-in-Publication Data

Hammond, J. R., 1951-
President Clinton and the working man / J.R. Hammond.
p.   cm.
ISBN 1-881320-32-4 : $10.00
1. Working class—Alabama—Political activity.  2. Coal miners—Alabama—Political activity. 3. Presidents—United States—Election—1992.
4. Hammond, J.R., 1951-   . I. Title.
HD8079.A2H36 1994
324.973'0928—dc20                                                94-39363
                                                                CIP

*The Black Belt, defined by its dark, rich soil, stretches
across central Alabama. It was the heart of the cotton
belt. It was and is a place of great beauty, of extreme
wealth and grinding poverty, of pain and joy. Here we
take our stand, listening to the past, looking to the
future.*

This book is dedicated
to working-class America

# Contents

# Part 3
## The 1992 Democratic National Convention

# Part 4
## The Campaign

# Part 5
## Aftermath

# Foreword

Life is funny. I know it's funny (as in humorous) but in an even more concrete vein, it can be funny/strange also. My life had been on an even keel for a number of years when I was taken out of my normal day-to-day existence and thrust into a level that would have left a lesser man reeling and staggering. This is an attempt to communicate to you my story. It was as though I experienced a lifetime of events compressed into a few short months. I hope you find it interesting reading. It sure made interesting living.

⌐

I could not have written this book without help from the following folks:

The gang at Dot's, Hie, Dot, and Mark;

The gang at Bud's, Bud, Gale, Peggy, Mr. & Mrs. Manderson;

The gang at the Korner Store;

The girls at Brookwood Sloss Federal and Russ;

My pals from Jim Walter #3 coal mine, Skeeter, Jimmy, Dennis, Riley, Steve, Dale, and Bill Thomas;

Ross Perot;

My close personal friends: James, Pete, Doug, Buddy, Roy, Carl, Roascoe, Mr. and Mrs. Wayne Terry, Randy the hess;

Jim and John, 2 true labor leaders;

My daughter Elesha, my Mom, Aunt Doris, Aunt Chris, Cousin Jimmy, and the rest of my family;

Renee, and her children Robby and Bridget;

For keeping me alive, Dr. Stephen Burge, Dr. Larry Gibbs, and the doctors at American Family Care in Irondale, Alabama.

And in Memoriam,

Miss Brandi Lee Poe, who rests with God.

# 1

# Comes The Working Man

# CHAPTER 1

## I Work For A Living

I am a coal miner. In 1992, I was also a 41-year-old, full-time, single parent doing my best to raise my 16-year-old daughter, Elesha Jade, in a stable, nurturing atmosphere conducive to all those factors that enable each of us to grow and, as those army commercials are so fond of saying, "Be all that you can be."

To give you a clearer understanding of who I am, and to enable you to better grasp how I was able to do what I did, I should drop back and fill in the picture of J. R. Hammond.

I was just one more baby boomer born in the summer of 1951. My mother was—swear to God—a coal miner's daughter. She was born Elizabeth Whalen, daughter of Tom and Annie Whalen.

She was born and raised in one of the company towns that were so prevalent during the 1930s in the Appalachian Mountain coal fields that north central Alabama had the fortune to be a part of. While it's true that most of the mountains themselves don't extend into Alabama, we do have some of the foothills, and the land is far from flat. And beneath this land lies coal.

Underground coal mining always has been dirty, dangerous work. The hazards are such that other aspects of life pale in comparison. This gives rise to the unity and brotherhood among mine workers that led to the start of the United Mine Workers of America and the rise of its illustrious leader, John L. Lewis.

My grandfather, Thomas S. Whalen, was a legend in the coal mines of Jefferson County, Alabama. When he was 31, in the year 1925, his left arm was cut off at the elbow in a mining accident. They buried his arm on the hill above the mine he worked in. He, supporting three children at the time, was off from work for a total of five weeks. He worked another 33 years in the depths of the coal mines with the use of only his right arm. He and Annie, my sweet granny, raised another seven children, one of whom was my dear mom.

My own father had almost no role in my childhood, as he and my mom were divorced before I was born. My grandfather had my mom move back home, so I came into the world with an extended family that included not only my mother, but also my grandfather and grandmother. I was raised in a blue-collar, union-oriented family, and I cut my teeth on tales of the Great Depression, Franklin Roosevelt, and John L. Lewis. All I ever knew growing up were working people. My mother became a working, single parent 30 years before it became fashionable.

My mother and I lived with my grandparents all the time I was growing up. We lived in one mine camp town after another until my grandfather retired. He then bought a home in a small place called Morgan's Chapel about 25 miles northwest of Birmingham, Alabama. I attended the local high school where I was not one of the "in" crowd, or on any of the school sports teams (slow of foot), but I did reasonably well in my academic endeavors. I graduated from high school in 1968. This is, of course, a watershed year in recent American political history. This was the year of the Chicago Democratic Debacle (read Convention) and nothing was ever the same again. There was so much going on all across the nation that year, I won't even attempt to cover it.

I was sort of a child of the Woodstock Nation, since I liked to wear the wild clothes. I went on to attend several colleges and finally graduated in 1974 from UAB—the University of Alabama in Birmingham. I ended up being a political science major with a minor in history. During my last two years in school, the Watergate scandal broke, and the world of abstract constitutional theories was transformed into a daily soap opera as all America watched what seemed like the entire Nixon administration give their version of events. It was, without a doubt, an exciting time in American history to be a student of politics. We would read about "separation of powers" in the textbook and then go home and hear the Nixon aides call out "Executive Privilege" and refuse to answer.

I went to work as a coal miner on July 29, 1974, at the Jim Walter Corporation #3 coal mine in Adger, Alabama. I still work there as this is being written, and I am writing this in my spare time. My daughter and I live in a manufactured home in central Alabama in the 7th Congressional District. We sort of take care of each other

*My campaign manager, Elesha Jade Hammond.*

here, and she worked closely with me as my campaign manager during the 1992 election.*

But I'll get to that shortly.

I go to work in the mine and she goes to school. If school happens to be out or it's summer she then does what a teenager normally does: go to the mall or the store, window shop, and a host of other things. She plays in the band at school, so I am a band parent going to all the games, parking cars for the Band Boosters, and doing the same kind of things for my daughter that most of you do for yours. But at the same time I'm holding down a 40-hours-a-week-plus job.

What I'm trying to say is I'm like you.

I wasn't involved in politics at all. I voted in every election and I had opinions, and I always leaned to the Democrats; but if they didn't field a good Presidential candidate, I did not consider myself bound to them. While I didn't vote Republican, I will tell you I sat out the presidential elections in 1984 and 1988. Any man who will

---

*Editor's Note:* Between the time J. R. finished his manuscript and its publication, he met and married Renee Rakestraw and he and Elesha moved with Renee and her children, Robbyn and Bridget, to nearby Woodstock, Alabama. He still works at the Jim Walter #3 mine.

tell the electorate in his nomination acceptance speech that he will raise their taxes, as Mondale did in '84, does not deserve to be President. Get real, man. Not a politically astute thing to do, I must say. And the loser of 1988, ol' tank-riding-Michael D., simply was not acceptable to the working people of this land.

So 1992 felt like the last hope for the rebuilding of the Democratic Party. And as I watched the working people of this nation being ignored, forgotten, and then attacked by the forces of Republican Big Money Politics, it occurred to me that the very way of life of the majority of working-class Americans was being threatened by the lack of a credible candidate for the 1992 elections.

Despite the fact that it was an incredible long shot, I decided to get involved and try to give the workers of this country at least one voice in the 1992 campaigns. Thus, the narrative that follows came about for two reasons: one, because I wanted to give you—the grassroots America that keeps this country going—a voice at the highest level, and two, I thought it would be cool for my daughter to see her old dad's name on the ballot. I try to do things that she will find of interest.

And believe you me, what happened became most interesting.

# CHAPTER 2

## Happy New Year

So it came to pass that on December 31st, 1991, I was speaking to my lovely and talented daughter, Elesha, about how 1992 was an election year and how the Presidential race was shaping up.

"Bush is in the same position as Hoover and Carter. I know you know most Presidents win reelection without a problem, but not this time. Despite the Desert Storm boost, he is in real trouble. One old political truism is that people vote their pocketbooks."

"Does that mean, Daddy, when times are bad, memories are short?"

"Yes, it means that the harder times are, the shorter the memory."

"Then who's going to be the next President, Daddy? Do you know?"

"It depends on who wins the Democratic nomination, I suppose. If the same crowd that has been running things wins out again, then Bush will go back in. Ex-Senator Paul Tsongas is already running, as is former California Governor Jerry Brown."

"Will one of them win the nomination? I thought you said anybody from the old group will lose to Bush. It doesn't make sense to nominate another loser."

"Right you are, little Darlin', it sure doesn't. That's why this is going to be a bad year for George Bush. There is another Democratic candidate that is markedly different from the others. For one thing, he's from the South. He's the Governor of Arkansas, Bill Clinton. I believe if it's handled right, he could make a real run at the White House."

"How will Bill Clinton get the nomination?"

"Well, all the big Democrats in the nation get together at the Democratic National Convention, and he has to get a majority of the delegates to vote for him and get the nod."

"How do they select all these delegates, Dad? Can anybody be one?"

"Each state has some kind of mechanism for delegate selection. The big elected Democratic leaders are automatically given some of each state's delegate spots, some are elected in a Party caucus or an outright general election. They even have a deal where if no one running as a delegate pledged to a certain group or individual gets enough votes to win outright, and if the group he represents gets at least 15 percent of the vote in a voting district, which in this case would be a Congressional District, then the top vote-getter for that group or candidate automatically gets a seat."

"I see, Daddy. Who runs for delegate?"

"As a whole, politicians, civic leaders, and those with money who are Party members become delegates. You have to have a real base of power to have any chance. Forty or 50 people run from each district, and most have a base of support before they try. Many are already elected officials on a local or county level. They win by getting concentrated support in their own home areas and combining this with a general random vote-getting among the areas they are not well known in. These are people who have part of their life invested in the Democratic Party. They give their support, time, and in many cases, money. These are your Capital-D Democrats. Most of the people in this country, however, aren't these kinds of people. They're what I am, a small-d democrat. We vote Democratic, but are too busy raising a family and holding down a job to become so involved. That's one reason working people are always getting the short end of the deal, because we don't have the time to go out and campaign and go to these National Conventions. The ones that do are already made and are not down here with the rest of the American workers, trying to raise our families and make ends meet. It's just not right."

"I'm sleepy Daddy. I'm going to bed now. Can we talk about this some other time?"

I said "sure" and kissed her good night. As I sat back on the couch watching the Times Square crowd get ready to celebrate the lowering of the big ball, I toyed with the idea of running for election to a delegate spot. I enjoy politics and actually had run once before. In fact, I nearly won a spot in 1980, just missing a runoff and losing out in the end to a person that held a statewide, elected position. I think he was on the State of Alabama Public Service Commission. I beat everybody but him, though.

My nickname at work in 1980 was Big Jim. In fact, I ran under the name "Big Jim" Hammond. The most famous Alabama governor (except for George Wallace) was a man named "Big Jim" Folsom. He was so well known as Big Jim that people didn't even use his last name. I knew that was why I did as well as I did, because I ran under the name "Big Jim" Hammond.

I knew that to have any shot at all—and if I was going to run I wanted to try to win—I would need some kind of hook, some kind of a gimmick. Boy, this was going to take some thought.

I needed something that would shine out among a list of 50 names. Something that would let the voters know I was not just like everyone else running. I am, after all, basically a coal miner. Coal Miner Hammond? No, that would limit my appeal. I wanted to run under a name that would tell at first glance who I was and what I was all about. I wanted the votes of every person that works for a living. I was just a working man that was trying to climb above the crowd and represent the working people of this nation.

It suddenly came to me. "Working Man" Hammond. Now there was an idea. Anybody that had enough nerve to run under the name "Working Man" Hammond would surely garner votes from regular types like myself. The more I thought about it, the more I liked it. And so as 1992 came busting onto the scene, a new political movement was born. I decided that I would run for delegate as an example to Elesha of how the system works. Maybe it would be just a one-man political movement, but hey, I was running so Elesha could see my name on the ballot and anything beyond that was icing on the cake.

"Working Man" Hammond. I liked it.

# CHAPTER 3

## John, I've Got An Idea

I spent the next few weeks in my normal routine of going to work, coming home, and taking care of Elesha. I was constantly thinking about running for delegate to the DNC under the name "Working Man" Hammond. I realized there was a good possibility I would not be well received by some members of the press and especially not well received by some members of the Democratic Party. I figured the odds of me actually winning were incalculable, but since I was only running so that Elesha could see my name on the ballot, a "good" showing on election day would have been quite sufficient.

But the more I thought about it, the more convinced I became that if I could get out the message to those people on my level that one of their own was in the race and would go up there and be a voice for them, then maybe I could pull off a political upset of sorts.

I belong to UMWA Local Union #928. The president of our 400-plus member Local is my good friend, John Stewart. John is one of these "born leader" types, and the Local was darn lucky to have him. He has since been elected President of UMWA District 20, which includes all of Alabama. He and I have talked over many things through the years, and politics has always been a prime topic.

At the beginning of February 1992, I decided to talk to John about my plans. As I came out of the mines that day, I dropped off my cap lamp and took a shower. I then approached John.

"How are you today, pal? Everything all right?"

He looked up from his work and said "J. R., is that you?"

Of course it was, and the palaver began.

"You know, John, this is an election year. If we don't get a good Democratic candidate to carry the banner, the Republicans will go in again."

"Yeah," John replied, "One more Mondale or Dukakis and they can forget ever going into the White House again. They have turned away from those that made the Party great and cater to those people too sorry to work and too liberal to care about working people."

"That's what I wanted to talk to you about. I had an idea the other night. I am going to run for delegate to the Democratic National Convention. But here's the idea I had, John. I'm not going to run under the name J. R. Hammond, or under the name 'Big Jim' Hammond, either. Listen to this: I'm going to run under the name, now get this, Working Man Hammond. What do you think?"

John smiled and looked amused. "Well, I must admit it is one I haven't heard before. So you're going to run for delegate to the Democratic Convention. Well, I'm on the UMWA Political Action Committee for the State of Alabama, and I'm going to see if I can get you an endorsement. It couldn't hurt."

"Great," I said, "That will give me immediate credibility. And running under a name like 'Working Man,' I'll need all the help I can get."

When I got home from work that day, I got on the phone and made the first of my many calls to Little Rock, Arkansas. I didn't bother to jot down the name of the guy I spoke to, but whoever it was did me a very big favor. I called the Clinton For President Committee and told whoever I got hold of that I was interested in running as a Clinton delegate here in Alabama's 7th Congressional District. He took my name and number and said they would get back to me. They never did. This turned out to be a break of unimaginable dimensions.

I next got on the phone to Alabama State Democratic headquarters to see what I needed to do to get on the ballot.

As it turned out, all I needed to do was sign a form, get it notarized and send it back in. Sounds simple enough, I thought, and thanked them for their time.

Sometime in mid-February I got my filing papers. When I began to read, I found there was a catch. At that time, if you wanted to run for delegate to the DNC you had three choices: one—you could run as a Clinton delegate; two—a Jerry Brown delegate, or three—there was a third choice—you could run as an uncommitted delegate.

I had not heard back from Little Rock, and even though I felt Clinton was the only Democrat that could win, I decided they didn't want me to run as a Clinton delegate—or maybe my name just got lost in the shuffle. I had decided to run as a Clinton delegate anyway but then my eyes scanned down to an asterisk at the bottom of the page beside a message that said something to this effect: While you can run as a delegate for any of the choices listed (Clinton, Brown, or Uncommitted) if a candidate doesn't want you to represent them, they can bounce you from the ballot.

"Whoa," I said to myself, "there's no way I'm going to let anybody from Arkansas keep my daughter from seeing my name on the ballot. So it looks like I'm now an Uncommitted delegate candidate." And so I put down that I wanted to run as an Uncommitted delegate candidate, and that I wanted my name to appear on the ballot as "Working Man" Hammond. The die was cast, and the stage was set for what was to be a wild election year for the country and for the household of J. R. and Elesha Jade Hammond.

# CHAPTER 4

## The Quest Begins

The last day to qualify for the June general election was March 7th. I waited until March 1st to send my papers in so that nobody would steal my idea. I felt that it was a uniquely American idea, an idea that while not on the level of $E=MC^2$ was pretty good for a coal miner.

After all, it symbolized what I had been doing the last 18 years, it symbolized who I was going to try and represent at the DNC, and it reflected who and what I was. But, most importantly, it symbolized the concept of working-class America.

The great forgotten majority of people in this country are working people who go to work every day, put in their eight or 10 or 12 hours, then come home and take care of their families. People who pay their taxes, support their local communities, and do the things that keep this nation going have no time to actually be involved in politics. They are too busy earning a living, raising their families, and paying their taxes. These are the people who take care of business in this country. They are not in some million-dollar board room making a fortune on some leveraged buy-out, nor are they buying some company just so they can close it down and use it for a tax write-off. I'm talking about Real America. Grass-roots America. Blue-collar, meat-and-potatoes America. Working-class America.

These Americans—not the President, not the Congress, not those in power, but people like myself, people like you—are the ones that keep this country going. It falls on our shoulders, and we have always shouldered it well. During the entire 200-plus years this nation has existed, the working people of this country have made the sacrifices that have kept the Stars and Stripes flying in the breeze. Sure, we complain from time to time, and election year is the only chance we get to voice our opinion.

You see, if you work for a living and raise a family, you don't have time to go out and riot just because something doesn't go your way. We are too busy earning a living and taking care of our families to become too involved in politics. In a real sense, for our children's sake, that's the way it's supposed to be. They need us to be there for them, and so we are.

We've always had a deal with "leaders" in this country. We don't mind doing what needs to be done. We elect leaders to run the country for us. We put our faith in them, and we put our trust in them. More than once we've been betrayed by those we elected, and we're used to a less than stellar performance by those we elect. Sometimes it seems we elect people who don't care about us. Working people know this all too well.

Anyhow, towards the end of March, the U.S. mail delivered a copy of my qualifying papers I had sent in. It showed I was now an official candidate and that "Working Man" Hammond was on the ballot. I didn't know it at the time, but I've since learned that the way I was listed on the ballot caused a lot of people to laugh over at Alabama State Democratic Headquarters. I suppose it was a real knee-slapper among some of the upper echelon there. It must have been amusing to think that an average guy, a full-time single parent trying to raise a teenage daughter would have the time, the energy, and the determination to become an active part of the democratic process.

I'm just a coal miner, but I'm a coal miner who cares about the land of my birth. I'm a coal miner who knew how to get on the ballot. And I'm a coal miner who felt that the working people in this country needed a voice at the DNC, even if I had to be the one to go there and be that voice. I had to try, anyway, for my daughter, and the sons and daughters all across America.

For how can those that don't do the hard physical labor, those who don't do the repetitive, mundane jobs day after day be expected to know what we think? They can't. They are on a level above us, and things that are important to us aren't necessarily important to them. Unless you work for a living in this country, you don't know what it's like, and you don't know how we feel.

After I had qualified and I was on the ballot, I commenced my word-of-mouth campaign. I would go up to people and ask them to vote for the Working Man. I didn't have a lot of time to go out and meet people, but I did what I could. The days passed, and everywhere I went I told them to vote for the Working Man.

I got my car tag in May, and as I was standing in line I talked politics to the others in line, asking them to vote for me and explaining I would give them a voice in the DNC. I called Democratic HQ with questions about the convention, and when I would tell them who I was, they would laugh. I called the local paper to see about an interview to help bolster my campaign and was told the delegate races were not important enough for press coverage.

I said okay, no problem.

When I told them who I was, the reporter I was talking with laughed and said, "So you're Working Man. We were wondering who you were." He had a goodly amount of amusement in his voice, and for the reasons already mentioned I could understand why.

In May, the official list of candidates was published. More than 40 people were running for five delegate positions. This was not surprising, but there was something about the list that made my head snap back so hard that whiplash set in. Out of 51 candidates for delegate from the 7th Congressional District, I was the only one to run as an Uncommitted delegate.

When I saw that was the case, I knew I could win. Not because I was a big name, or because my "Working Man" Hammond listing leapt off the page at the voters, and not because I was being endorsed by the UMWA (My good friend John Stewart was able to get this endorsement for me after all). No, I knew I could win because I had some help from a quite unexpected source. You see, it turned out there was this little guy from Texas, and, well, he loved uncommitted people. Through an unlikely and ironic political twist, I, as an Uncommitted delegate candidate, was backed by H. Ross Perot. All of a sudden, being the only Uncommitted candidate running became very interesting.

# CHAPTER 5

## Ross, I Owe You One

Please allow me to digress a moment while I explain to you the significance of a Texas billionaire on my life.

I don't know what propels people towards their destiny. I don't think anyone does. Perhaps as in making a tree, only God is privy to the ebb and flow of life's undercurrents that ultimately lead us to our destination. I only know that I owe Mr. Ross Perot.

For when Ross Perot decided that he would allow his name to be put on the ballot in all 50 states, he had no idea that he was directly impacting the political life of a grass-roots American coal miner. Not only did Mr. Perot make a mark in American political history, but he actually put one of the people he was trying to help in a position where we seldom get to be. He was rocking the boat, politically speaking, on a nationwide scale.

I firmly believe that Ross Perot was only doing what any man-of-the-people in his position would do. He was doing the same thing I was trying to do. We were trying to put in positions of power people with a real concern for working-class American citizens. At the time of the 1992 DNC, he and I both had six-month-old political careers. There is evidence that while both of us made some mistakes, we both came out of the election in an elevated position. He, of course, is set for another run at the White House. I imagine that he and the group he has founded, United We Stand, will become a factor in American politics for as long as he wants it to be.

Ross Perot spent $16 million of his own money putting the idea of a Perot presidency in the minds of the American people. Why he decided to tell people to vote uncommitted in the Democratic primaries starting in March of '92, only he knows. But I can tell you this, Ross Perot, if I ever get the chance to thank you personally, consider it done.

His contribution to the political arena was so significant that it is vastly underrated by the political pundits of both parties. He really touched a nerve with the blue-collar crowd.

I have worked in the mines going on 20 years, spent the better part of it talking to the people I work with, and believe me we've talked about everything under the sun. Close to 1,000 different people must have worked at that mine while I've been there, and I must have said something to each one of them. When you work in a frontier atmosphere like a coal mine, the walls of civilization—the face that people wear in the office, the face that people wear on the street, the polished veneer that is the face of civilization—are stripped away, and you hear what people really think.

I have learned more about what people think by eating lunch with them than any poll-taker could find out from a survey. If you want to know what people think, don't give them a questionnaire to fill out; eat lunch with them in a coal mine. Twenty years of listening to what people say about this country is one of the things that gave me the credibility to call myself the Voice of the Working People all through the DNC and the campaign. I have learned to appreciate differences of opinion as a fact of life.

The top leaders of the Democratic Party didn't hear what we said about Carter, Mondale, and Dukakis, but I did. I know what people thought of how Reagan handled things and how much different the feelings were about Bush. And from what I heard— mark my words well—if it had been any other Democrat than Clinton running in 1992, Bush would have beaten him badly. Only a moderate Son of the South could have beaten the Republicans. Running two moderate Southerners on the Democratic ticket was almost unfair. I hope that the leadership of the Party will recognize the only course to follow is a policy of moderation. Working people won't settle for less.

The working people in this country have been in a quandary for some time now, and they have been looking for someone to lead them. I hoped that you, President Clinton, would be the one to show this nation the way out of the dark and into the light. And I know about being shown the way back into the light.

Once I was working on a water pump off in old section way back in the mine where people rarely go. It was the first time I had been back there, and I was unfamiliar with the area. I had fixed the pump and was going back to the more traveled areas of the mine when I took a wrong turn and BAM!, I was as lost as a man could be. Deep water everywhere, bad top, rocks hanging down. A person could get killed. It took them nearly three hours to find me and I promise you that was a long three hours. As a matter of fact, I was rescued by my cousin, Jimmy Higginbotham. Thanks, Cuz.

I was definitely glad to see him. Being lost in a coal mine area for three hours will make you think you'll never get out alive. That's the way many people feel about themselves. They have been waiting to be a part of things again, and I deeply hope President Clinton can figure out how to bring them in.

I spent three hours lost and waiting to be found. To keep myself occupied, I spent the time thinking up things one could do while lost in a mine. Here's the list I jotted down while I was waiting for them to find me.

### "WORKING MAN" HAMMOND'S TOP 10 LIST OF THINGS TO DO WHILE LOST IN A COAL MINE

#10—Wander around aimlessly until panic sets in
#9—Assign pet names to timbers and lumps of coal
#8—Sing the song "Miller's Cave"
#7—Write letter to congressman about lax "Lost In Coal Mine Laws"
#6—Keep telling yourself "They'll find me, they'll find me"
#5—Make a list of things to do if you ever get out, or of people to get even with
#4—See how long you can go without food and water
#3—Tell life story to a passing bat
#2—Decide church wasn't that boring after all
#1—Hope you don't die


I hope you found a little amusement in that. It sure wasn't a pleasant way to spend a morning.

I wrote this chapter just to thank H. Ross Perot, and it seems I drifted a little. You try working into a conversation a top 10 list of things to do while lost in a coal mine. It isn't easy.

Anyway, Ross Perot, you did an incredible job getting grassroots America off their tails and into the habit of voting.

Mr. Perot had the public voting uncommitted all through the months of March, April, and May. Every primary drew 25 percent to 35 percent uncommitted voters' tallies. I knew all I had to do was get 15 percent in the 7th District, and I was headed to New York

City. June 2nd drew nearer and nearer, and I knew I had a shot at it in a big way. I held my breath and it was on the morning of June 2nd that I woke up with a smile on my face. Let it happen, "Captain." I went to work and afterwards I came back out and I got cleaned up and headed for home. I had one stop to make on the way home. I had to go and vote for myself—my all-time favorite candidate.

# CHAPTER 6

## Little Old Ladies

June 2nd, 1992, was a turning point in my life. The month of May that led up to that fateful day was charged with the energy of democracy at work. Everywhere I went, I would ask people to vote for me by saying "vote for the Working Man" and shake their hand. I got to be real good at it, too.

At work, people were genuinely happy that I was running—some of them, anyway. I got tremendous feedback, and people were glad to know somebody who might end up a "political leader." To working people at our level of involvement, which is to say not involved at all, knowing anybody in politics means you're a leader of sorts.

I had not been able to get any press exposure because nobody gave me any kind of a chance. I suppose they couldn't imagine a normal person being able to make much headway in this unique realm of political royalty. I suppose the idea of grass-roots political action was so alien to politics that members of the press didn't know what a factor it could be.

I had to stop and vote on "Super Tuesday" at the Bucksville, Alabama, Baptist Church. This polling place is manned by a group of the most precious senior ladies you ever saw. When I came in and registered to vote, I mentioned that I was the Working Man, and they had noticed me on the ballot. They said they were sorry I hadn't told them sooner or they would have helped. I told them not to worry because I was going to win anyway, so it didn't matter.

And I was right. Out of over 50 people running, my name was last on the ballot at the end of the middle column of candidates' names and all the way nearly flush with the bottom of the page—we use paper ballots at my polling place. I mean, you had to strain to see that my name was actually on the list. I ended up with 8,221 votes.

I would like to have seen just how many I would have gotten if I had been first instead of last.

Anyway, I voted, and then I went home to watch the results come in. On the way home I went by the stores where I had campaign signs posted.

I told you about my campaign signs, didn't I? Back in early May I had budgeted $10 for campaign material. I ended up with five posterboard signs—white with red lettering. They looked like this:

VOTE
FOR
WORKING
MAN
HAMMOND
DELEGATE DEMO CONVENTION
UMWA
ENDORSED

I had five of these signs made by my campaign staff—my campaign staff was my daughter Elesha. Four were stolen or lost, and one is presently at rest beneath my bed. I would have hated losing after personally spending my own cash for the campaign material. Ten bucks is ten bucks. I can imagine how Ross Perot must feel.

The polls closed at 7 p.m., and the networks started putting out predictions at 9 p.m. Alabama was first, and Uncommitted was pulling down around 25 percent of the vote in Alabama. If my own District was following the trend, and I was sure that it would, I had ridden home a long shot of 100,000 to 1 because five people were elected out of a Congressional District with a population of 500,000.

I called the local paper to see if they had any numbers. They told me I was carrying only 7 percent and it would take about 15 percent to win. As it turned out, if I had been anything besides an Uncommitted candidate my total of 8,221 votes would not have gotten me elected as a delegate.

I was unable to get any official information that night, so I went to work on Wednesday not actually knowing the outcome. The bathhouse was abuzz about whether or not I had won. I told them one guy told me I lost, but said it wasn't official.

I felt sure I had won because of the wide appeal that Ross Perot

*Outside campaign headquarters.*

had attached to voting uncommitted. All the news programs on Monday night, June 1st, showed people being told by Perot workers to vote uncommitted. And of course, the main reason I felt sure I had won was because I am in touch with the working people of this land. I have worked in the coal mines for almost 19 years, and I am a full-time, single, band parent. My life revolves around my daughter, just like the millions of other parents whose lives revolve around their children. I shop for groceries, wash clothes, clean house, cook meals, help my daughter in her studies when she asks me to, and let her be herself. I am just an average American worker with a family to raise and bills to pay. I know what life is like in America in 1994, and I knew about life in America in 1992. I just knew I had won.

Earlier, the last week in May, I had received a card from the State of Alabama Democratic Party saying if I didn't win I had to call headquarters and register in order to be considered for the At-Large delegate election to be held at the June 6th meeting in Birmingham. So when I got home, I called Democratic Party headquarters to see if they had any vote totals, and they told me they didn't. I said I wanted to register for the At-Large delegate election to be held on Saturday.

This is where the story gets a little more exciting.

The guy I was talking with told me how it worked: "You have to run pledged to the same candidate that you did in the election. If you ran as a Clinton delegate, you have to run again for Clinton—and the same for Brown, too."

I said, "I didn't run as either. I ran as an Uncommitted delegate from the 7th District. As a matter of fact, I was the only Uncommitted delegate running in the 7th District."

He said, "Is this the Working Man?"

"Yes, it is."

"And you say you were the only person that ran as an Uncommitted delegate?"

"Yes, I was," I said, with a definite touch of "laugh at me now, how about it," in my voice.

He blurted out, "In that case, you've won! Wait a minute, let me check the preference vote totals to be sure, but I know your district was running well over that. Yes! Here it is, 21 percent. Congratulations, Working Man!"

I thanked him for his troubles and hung up the phone. Well, now. What do you know? What do you think? What do I do now?

I knew what to do. I called the local paper, *The Tuscaloosa News*, and spoke to the reporter that I had tried to get to interview me before the election.

"Hi. This is the Working Man. Do you have any vote totals on the delegate races?"

"No, I sure don't. Sorry."

"Well, I've got one for you. I won. I'm the first one in the state to know I won. Because of the big uncommitted vote, I'm headed to NYC."

He wanted to interview me for the Sunday paper. I agreed to meet with him at my house after the big meeting on Saturday. I knew I'd have to deal with the press sometime, and I might as well start as soon as possible.

It looked like I was going to have a big ol' time this weekend. This was the big meeting—where I would meet all the Big Cats in Alabama, where the Working Man would begin his role as The Voice of the Working Person in the National Democratic Party. Was this cool or what?

# CHAPTER 7

## A Century Dies

My 1986 Buick Century ran hot on the way home from work yesterday. I think it blew the head gasket or cracked the block. I hope it was the gasket, but with my luck it will be the block.

Actually, I can't complain about my luck because I have custody of my daughter and know the President. But I'm getting ahead of my tale.

After I called the reporter and arranged an interview for the Saturday after my meeting with the Democratic Party hierarchy, I got on the phone to everyone I knew. I called my mom, my aunts, my friends, even people I wasn't sure liked me at all. Excited? No, not me. I then got in my car and drove to the stores where I had put the signs up and told them about my being elected. I called my friend John Stewart, and it was my time to blurt out something: "John, you won't believe it! I won! I won!"

He coolly replied, "Well that's great, J. R., way to go." John is a man of keen vision and knew it would be of immense value to the working people of this country to have one of us there at the DNC.

On Thursday when I went to work, the bathhouse where we change into our work clothes quickly became a beehive of talk as I came through and told them I had won. Some were actually disappointed when I told them I was headed to NYC. One guy said, "I thought you said you lost." I told him it was one of the great political upsets in history, and the person that told me I lost was "wishful-thinking his way, and his wish didn't come true." It was a very exciting day for a regular-type person like myself and turned out to be just one of many. I had no idea just how quickly one big moment after another would come.

On Saturday, June 6th, 1992, I had to attend the State Democratic Party meeting in Birmingham. I knew no one in the Party, so it was a learning experience. I got there when I was told to, and, of course, I was the last one to arrive.

I went in to watch the proceedings, and I saw a table where people were signing in and getting those stick-on name tags that say "Hello, my name is..." and you write your name in the blank spot. When I told them who I was, I could tell someone had been talking about me because the person handling the sign-in told me they had been wondering if I would show up. I wrote "Working Man" Hammond on my tag and went inside the actual conference room where the Alabama State Democratic Party Executive Committee was meeting to elect At-Large Delegates to bring up the number of women and minorities to the correct number.

I saw an empty chair and sat down. In the chair were ballots with the names of some of the people running for the open spots. When I looked at the list on one ballot, there were 15 names and every one of them was a big wheel in Alabama state politics. Most were state senators or ex-senators and only one of them would be elected. There was a list of people already elected, and it was the first list I had seen of just who besides myself would be going to the DNC. It was a list of "Who's Who" in Alabama politics.

As I sat there realizing I was the only ordinary person there, I felt a tap on my shoulder. I looked up into an angelic face. She said, "Mr. Hammond, these chairs are for the Executive Committee only. You'll have to move." I moved out of the room and went out in the lobby. People started coming up to me and introducing themselves—leaders, people that run the state on an everyday basis, movers and shakers and their aides. It seemed like everyone there was somebody, except me. While at the time it seemed like a big deal, it was nothing to what would come later.

I met a good many of the people going to the DNC that day and discovered one other thing. There were 67 delegates going to the DNC from Alabama, and I was the only one not officially saying I was going to vote for Bill Clinton. I thought about it and immediately decided that if I wanted any input I had better be a Clintonite from the word Go. I had wanted to be a Clinton delegate anyway, so I told some reporter I had decided to vote for Clinton before I left there. He was from a local radio station with an all-talk format, and I was already a frequent caller to the early morning talk show and the 4 p.m. sports talk show on this station. I ended up doing a full-blown interview with him before I went home. He told me it would be aired the following Monday. It was, too.

I called the *Tuscaloosa News* reporter and he came to my house late that afternoon. I told him about myself, my being raised by my one-armed grandfather, and the fact that I was going to do my best to represent the working people of this nation.

I also told him about how the meeting went, how everyone there was a big wheel except me, and how things had been generally fine and dandy. I told him I was now an official Bill Clinton man, and how my main concern was to help bring to the Democratic Party the moderate direction it had been lacking for twelve years.

He took a picture of me holding up a campaign poster produced by my campaign staff—like I said, my staff consisted of my daughter and her father—and he left. He didn't know if it would make the Sunday paper because of the lateness of the hour.

The next day I got up and went to see if I made the Sunday paper. I walked up to the paper box and when I got close enough, I could see my picture in color on the front page. I was the feature on the front page of Section B of the paper, and they used my picture on the front page as a teaser. The caption read, "Working Man goes to Big Apple. Story inside."

There was a big color picture inside on page B1 of me holding my sign and a big line of print over it that read, "Improbable Winner heads to NYC for the DNC." Or something to that effect. It did say "improbable winner" exactly. All the people that live around me read it, and everybody I talked to was happy one of them had made it this far into the political process.

Remember, I was not a capital-letter Democrat. I was not in politics at all yet. I had won an election in a Congressional-sized district. I was quite content with this one newspaper story, and I had no intention at that time to make a big deal of what I had done. I got several copies of that paper and still have one here somewhere. It was a good story.

The reporter called one of the leaders of the Democratic Party, who told him I was a real hit at the big meeting in Birmingham. Funny, I couldn't tell it at the time. Well, maybe a little. Those people are not used to being around ordinary folks.

It would have been easy to have spent my time at the convention and the campaign walking around with my mouth open saying "Gollee" like Gomer used to on the "Andy Griffith Show." But I decided that since I represented the working people of America, I had an honored responsibility and, by gosh, I was not going to let you people down. I would not back down from anybody, and I was going to carry myself in a manner that would bring no dishonor to those whose torch I was proud to bear—you people that make up the bulk of the population and do all the actual work in the country; not the big cats, not the CEOs, and not those who are already in a position where they have personal access to the political process. No, I was going to champion only those who work for a living, those who are retired, those who are disabled and unable to work, and, finally, with a passion born of my fatherless childhood, I was going to do what I could for the children of this country.

I went to bed with a good feeling. I had just been in politics for five days and was already known as a champion of the middle class. I felt so at ease doing radio and newspaper interviews that I began to think maybe I was cut out for this kind of stuff. It was a good thing, too, because in a very short time I was going to be involved at a level I would never have dreamed of, and since I represented you I had to do a good job of it. On Monday morning I decided to call the talk radio station I mentioned earlier and surprise the hosts with the news of my election. Instead, they surprised me.

# CHAPTER 8

## I Heard It Through The Grapevine

The article in *The Tuscaloosa News* Sunday paper on June 7, 1992, was an interesting piece of journalism for several reasons. Of course, as its subject I found it fascinating and of great depth and insight. I guess when you first see a big story about yourself in a newspaper it can be a heady experience. I handled it well enough, I suppose, if you don't count me carrying around a copy of the paper and showing it to people that hadn't seen it. Showing it to all the people I knew in all the stores around here wasn't too bad, I guess. When I started stopping total strangers and showing it to them, I realized perhaps I was overdoing it.

Like I mentioned earlier, I was a regular caller on this early morning talk show. I would call in and present poems I had written, go into a humorous monologue I had written, or just engage in snappy banter with the hosts. I have since had a falling out with them over—of all things—politics. But we were still tight on June 8th, 1992.

I got up early that Monday morning so I would have time to call in before I went to work that day. I had really had a good call-in relationship with this radio station—including one call where I phoned the afternoon talk show host shortly after I had qualified to run under the name Working Man. It went something like this:

Host: "And now we have one of our regular callers, J. R. from Woodstock. How are you, J. R.?"

Me: "Just fine. I'm calling today about the upcoming election in June. I had an idea about running for office under a name other than a person's given name. You know, like a few years ago when that guy had his name illegally changed to 'None Of The Above' and tried to run under that name?"

Host: "Yes, I remember that. What were you thinking of, in particular?"

Me: "Well, I was thinking about running for delegate to the Democratic National Convention under a name that would not only tell the voters when they looked at the ballot who I am, but would also tell them what I am and what I stand for. A name that would convey immediately and at first glance that I was the candidate they could get behind because I was more like them than anyone else running. A name like—oh, let's see, yes, a name like Working Man Hammond. Indeed, I think if I were to run under a name like Working Man Hammond, I could get the vote of the working people of this great state and win in a cake walk. What do you think?"

Host: "Well, I guess you're right J. R. It's too bad the Democratic Party won't let you run under this name."

Me: "Have I got some news for you, pal. I have already qualified to run under the name "Working Man" Hammond and will appear as such on the June 2nd ballot. Pretty clever, eh?"

Host: "Yes, and it was pretty slick how you worked in a campaign spot there, also. I guess you owe us for it, too."

Me: "Just write the bill in the dust and we'll let the rain settle it. Talk to you later."

So some people found out I was running by listening to that show that afternoon. I have talked to people who actually heard me that day, and they were amused at the fact I was able to slip an impromptu advertisement by the host. Before I forget, and despite the fact it is well out of chronological order, let me insert the last poem I did on this morning talk show, the day before I left to go to NYC for the DNC.

THE DELEGATE

I can't hide my elation
at my situation

I beat back rejection
and won my election

It is my intention
at the Democratic Convention

To represent thosen
by whom I was chosen

The voters made their choice
now I must be their voice

I promise to do all that I can
yours sincerely, Working Man

I wanted to put that down before it slipped my mind. Pardon the digression, but I hope you enjoyed it. I meant it, too. Every word of it. In fact, taking my role too seriously was a real problem for me. I'm going to leave this subject now, but I promise to get back to it later.

Let's see, where was I?

June 8th, 1992, around 6 a.m. I was calling the show to tell the co-hosts about my election and my going to the big meeting and the big spread in *The Tuscaloosa News*. I started out by saying "hello" and telling them "I had a real surprise for them."

They said, "You won your race and are going to the Democratic National Convention."

I said, "How do you know that?" and their answer was remarkable. They said a story about my election was on the front page of that morning's *Birmingham Post-Herald*, our daily morning newspaper around and about the Magic City (Birmingham's colorful nickname). I was shocked! Apparently, *The Tuscaloosa News* story had been put on the wire and was carried by many papers—and other media—all over the country!

Every paper in Alabama must have carried the story in some form because all the papers I checked with did. That story was all about my being an average guy with an opportunity to go where the average nonpolitical working-class guy had never been before, what a hit I was at the state meeting the past Saturday, and all the high aspirations I had about being the voice of working-class America at the DNC.

It is hard to express the feelings one has going to work knowing your name and story are splashed all over the front page of the paper. Needless to say I felt pleased with myself, and not just for the ego-trip reason that readily leaps out if you think about it.

No, I felt good because I now had a real chance to champion those issues we working people hold so dear: getting a fair shake from the government on our taxes, getting some form of health care for those poor people making minimum wage, taking the tax burden off the backs of the working class, and taking back the stranglehold over our lives that the Republicans had during the years of Democratic noncandidates for President.

Needless to say when I got to work I got cheers from my supporters and friends, and looks of disbelief from the rest.

Everywhere I went in the mine that day, I was congratulated and slapped on the back. I went home that evening in great spirits and full of the love of democracy.

I had a stray thought about how I would have to handle myself at the Convention, and was filled with an amazing sense of calm and resolve. I was going to go up there and fight for American workers everywhere.

I had a message to carry, and all I needed was a tall enough soapbox to stand on, and the people of Alabama—indeed, the nation—would know that at least one working person had made a breakthrough.

Little did I know how soon that soapbox would be coming my way.

# CHAPTER 9

## June 10th, 1992, And You Are There

When I went in to work the next day, it followed on the heels of a very special night. Everyone I knew must have read the paper and called me that night. I was starting to get excited about the possibilities that presented themselves to me.

I got to work early that morning and before I put on my work clothes I put up a copy of the newspaper article on the UMWA bulletin board. As I finished dressing, everybody on the 11 to 7 shift read the article and came by to say "OK, pal, way to go!" There's a lot of actual camaraderie in the mines because of the closeness of the situation on the job. All the people on the day shift that had missed the article the day before were looking at the headlines when I walked by. Again, it is a great experience to have your peer group behind you in a big way. It makes all the effort seem worthwhile.

I went to a part of the mine called #7 Section, which translates loosely as "We have to call this area something. #7 Section is as good a name as any, so let's call it that!" I worked hard all day servicing machinery, doing oil changes, lube jobs, fluid level checks, that sort of thing.

Let me explain right now that I have an adversarial relationship with my employer. The management at my coal mine and I are not friends. Many of you know what it's like to have the boss after you all the time. On-the-job antagonism from your employers is stressful. I mention this because around 2 p.m. I heard my name being called out over the mine paging system. I walked over and picked up the phone. It was the CO monitor room attendant calling, and he told me to come by the personnel office after I got cleaned up.

As I said, I am not friends with the management and had suffered several "invitations" like this before. These were meetings where I was subjected to punishing attacks on my person and threats of the loss of my livelihood and that of my daughter. I know they don't like me and I don't like them. So when I was called to the phone and told I had a meeting after work, the first thing I said was, "I didn't do it. I didn't do anything, and they want to have a meeting about it? And if I did do it, I have an explanation. I'm innocent, I tell you."

I was telling this to the boss on #7 Section. I then asked the CO room man, "Do I need to carry a union representative with me? What is it about?" He said, "No, you don't need a union rep. They want to talk to you about being on TV tomorrow."

I liked this. A chance to be an actual voice for the American worker. I said I'd be there by around 3:15. It was looking like I might end up more involved in this political thing than I ever thought. I figured if I went over well on the show, it would give me a leg up on that soapbox I was looking for.

I came out of the mine and got cleaned up. I went back into unfriendly territory, boss territory, and went in the room where the personnel manager was waiting.

*"Channel 13 wants you to do a live talk show tomorrow morning. Call this number. The mine manager is going to let you off from work, so it's no problem."*

This was strange. The mine manager and I were not friends, and I couldn't imagine why he would be doing me a favor. I called the station, and was told I was wanted for the opening segment of a local talk show the next morning. It was to be about a five minute interview, and we were to talk about my election and upcoming trip to the DNC in NYC. I agreed and had to be there at 7:30 a.m., dressed out and ready to talk.

I went back through the bathhouse and word had already spread about the TV show. Almost everyone was wishing me well and saying they would set their VCRs to record it. My friends were very happy for me and gave me the traditional "break a leg" salute.

I went home and for the third time in one week called everyone I knew to tell them I was going to be on the tube the next day. It was nice calling people with good news. I had a chat with my daughter about it and she was visibly underwhelmed, but decided it would be cool to go to a TV station and see a live broadcast. We made plans to leave early and be there in plenty of time to get a feel for the situation.

I really didn't have any idea what I would say, but I also didn't have any fear or nervousness or qualms or even misgivings about agreeing to do the show.

I was still puzzled why the bosses gave me the day off to go and do a live TV interview. My excitement at possibly making an impact on the people of Alabama made getting sleep nearly impossible. I think around 3 a.m. I finally dozed off. I knew one thing: I would speak my mind and tell them why this was the year of the Democratic Party in America.

6 a.m. came and I started getting ready to go to the TV station. I felt calmer than someone not used to this sort of thing had a right to feel. I was not alone, for I represented all the normal people nationwide who were not involved in politics, yet we did our jobs, took care of our families, paid our taxes and voted every election— we who normally don't get a chance to express ourselves on the screen. It was as though I was meant to go on that show, and I was ready for it. I still had no idea what I was going to say, but I meant to be precise, concise, and erudite (that means scholarly, I'm told).

We drove to the station and met the two co-hosts in time to become comfortable with them. They finally put me in a chair, and one of the hosts was going to start the interview by holding up the campaign sign I had brought along at their request. The show was supposed to last five minutes. I guess they thought they were going to talk to a hick or something, what with me calling myself "Working Man" and all. I guess I am compared to some circles. But I don't think I came across like a hick. Here, you can judge for yourself.

TRANSCRIPT OF MY FIRST INTERVIEW LIVE AND IN PERSON ON A LOCAL MORNING TV TALK SHOW

Host: (Holding up my campaign sign) "You may or may not have seen this campaign sign during the last election: Vote for Working Man Hammond, United Mine Workers of America Endorsed. Four were made, two were stolen, and only one of them survived the campaign."

Hostess: "J. R. Hammond decided this year he would run for a position as a delegate to the Democratic National Convention. His 16-year old daughter was his campaign manager and lo and behold J. R. will be going to the Democratic Convention in just a few weeks now. He joins us on "Top Of The Morning" to talk about his successful campaign. Congratulations, first of all."

Working Man: "Good morning. What a country, huh?"

Host: "Yes, it is still a pretty good country when a working man, which is how you describe yourself—you work in the deep mines there in Adger—can do something."

Working Man: "I work about 1,300 feet deep. I want to thank all the members of UMWA local 1928 who have supported me so far and the president, John Stewart. He's been a big help. It's been a real interesting spring."

Hostess: "I was going to say, starting back in February when you first decided you would run as a delegate and put your name on the ballot, at that point in time what was going through your mind?"

Working Man: "I said to myself, well, as big a long shot as it is, I have a lot better chance of winning if I'm on the ballot than if I'm not on the ballot."

Host: "A lot of other folks wanted to be a delegate, but they ran as a Clinton delegate or a Brown delegate on the Democratic ballot . . ."

Working Man: "Clinton and Brown."

Host: "No one else thought of running Uncommitted?"

Working Man: "I don't know why they didn't, but I did."

Hostess: "At that point you had not made your decision about—"

Working Man: "Who I was going to support? No, I was going to wait and see what developed during the primary season. When Clinton went to the front, I watched him in particular. Of course, I keep track of what's going on, anyway. Clinton's the man this time. I'm going to vote for him on the first ballot even though I was elected Uncommitted. He's going to win in November. I'm behind Clinton 100 percent."

Hostess: "It's interesting though, isn't it, that Clinton's not the one that secured your spot."

Working Man: "Ross Perot."

Hostess: "You know that most people that checked that Uncommitted box were casting their vote for Ross Perot."

Working Man: "Yes, ma'am. I was watching the news on Monday and they showed a clip from Perot headquarters and they were telling everyone that called in to vote Uncommitted, and I thought that this could turn out to be a very interesting election."

Host: "You personally got 8,000 votes . . ."

Working Man: "8,221. I got the fewest votes of any elected delegate in the state. I won because I was the only one who ran Uncommitted."

Host: "In the whole state?"

Working Man: "In the 7th Congressional District, so I got all the

Uncommitted vote. Hey, I'll take it."

Hostess: "You had your first meeting this past Saturday with all of the other delegates that will be going to the Convention."

Working Man: "The big wheels, the movers and shakers in the state of Alabama."

Hostess: "Everybody else was a lawyer or a leader in the Party."

Working Man: "Lawyers, politicians, and me. It was something."

Host: "Were they nice to you?"

Working Man: "They were real cordial. Some of them came by and introduced themselves to me. It was a real interesting experience. Now, I'm looking forward to representing the working people of America as best I can."

Host: "What's the closest you've been to New York?"

Working Man: "I've been to Chicago one time. No, I used to lobby for the UMWA in Washington, D.C., in the mid-seventies and helped pass the Black Lung Bill in '77."

Host: "So are you excited about going?"

Working Man: "I'm looking forward to helping reshape the Democratic Party, to get it more in the middle of the road, to become more moderate. That's what's been wrong with the Democratic Party, they've lost the working people by being too far left of center. The coalition FDR built in 1932 consisted of working people, women, and minorities. The disenfranchised, so to speak. That's why the Republicans have been winning, because working people have been voting for them and not for us. If I have any say-so about it, we'll get the Party back in the middle of the road, get the votes of the working people, and win in November."

Hostess: "You think Bill Clinton can do that?"

Working Man: "I sure do."

Host: "You keep talking about it, and we were talking before the show where you made a good point about the last election, and if you'd care to make it again now. . ."

Working Man: "Four years ago, Dukakis had a big lead over George Bush. It's a long time to November, a lot could happen. Hilary's going to be a big boost—Mrs. Clinton. She's real concerned with child care. That's one of the problems in this country, child abuse, child neglect. Everybody knows it. She started the Arkansas Child Abuse Program."

Hostess: "J. R., Ross Perot is grabbing a lot of headlines now. First of all, how do you think the public's going to react to Ross Perot and second, how is Bill Clinton going to steal the limelight away from him?"

Working Man: "Right now, the man is having a free ride—no tough questions to answer, and no hard decisions to make. But this is the way I look at it: You tell me how a man with $3.5 billion can relate to what kind of life the working people in this country have to live. George Bush is the same way. He went to a grocery store and had never seen a laser price scanner before. He didn't know what it was. How can these people relate to what working people are all about?"

Host: "Will you be active in the campaign when you come back? Will you and your union brothers be actively supporting Clinton?"

Working Man: "I believe so. I think that this is the year Bill Clinton pulls the coalition back together, gets working people back involved in the Democratic Party, and we'll win in November."

Host: "Did you see him do the 'Today Show' yesterday? It was one of the best public appearances I've seen him do. No, you were at work, weren't you?"

Working Man: "A lot of people made a big deal because he was playing saxophone on the 'Arsenio Hall Show.' He is a man of the people, not some stuffed-shirt politician. He's a real man, a man of the people, he'll get the Democratic Party back in midstream and win in November."

Hostess: "J. R., good luck."

Host: "Congratulations, J. R. You'll be staying at the Loews Hotel with the rest of the delegation. It's very nice, J. R., you're going to like it. Let me get this in. I know we're running short on time. You are raising money, and it'll cost around $1,500 to go. How can people help if they want to?"

Working Man: "If anyone wants to help, they can send it to J. R. Hammond, Woodstock, Alabama. If they want to help, I'll appreciate it. If not, I'll raise the money anyway because I'm going to go up there and do what I can for the working people of this country."

Host & Hostess: "Thanks for being here."

Working Man: "You're welcome."

Well, there you have it. I left the station feeling like I had done a good job. Upon review of the tape of the show, I reached several conclusions: I could handle myself in any situation because nothing contains more potential pitfalls than live TV; I knew what I was talking about when I spoke of the issues concerning working people; I sure was glad I had a history minor to go with my political science degree; and I had to find a different word besides "interesting" because I ended up using the word five times during the interview.

When I went into one of the local stores after I got home that day, I was greeted by a chorus of applause by those there who had watched the show. It was a very satisfying experience, on the whole. And one last thing before I press on—remember I said I couldn't figure out why the management there at the mine let me off that day? When I went by there to get my paycheck, I ran into the big bosses there. The head boss said, "I saw the show. You didn't do near as bad as I thought you would. If you want to see it, we have it recorded." Then I knew why they let me off that day. They thought I would make a fool of myself on live TV, and they wanted a recording of it. I fooled them instead.

I had a feeling after this that I had a chance to make a real impact in this political game. After all, I was being called Working Man already. Any kind of a break and I could be a high-profile delegate in NYC. As it turned out, I didn't have long to wait. By the weekend of July 4th, I was smokin'.

# CHAPTER 10

## Not Just An Ordinary Delegate

The interview was a big success. I carried copies of the video tape everywhere. I called the head of the Clinton campaign here in Alabama, Mr. John Saxon, and went by his office to see him. I asked him to watch it, and he was impressed enough to put me on the Clinton for President Campaign Alabama State Steering Committee. This and a dollar will get you a cup of coffee here in Alabama; it will not some places in New York. Still, it was nice to be able to tell people you were on the Clinton for President Campaign Alabama State Steering Committee. Only the elite and powerful were on it, except, of course, for me.

I spent the next two weeks going about my business, going to work like any normal person, and coming home in the evenings taking care of my daughter. Of course, I noticed some changes in my life. My mail became a potpourri of politically pertinent parcels. Snuck a bit of alliteration in on you, didn't I? I got mail from groups all over the nation, for some things and against others. I received a brochure from the trucking people, the Israeli lobby, and a big letter from the supporters of one guy currently in the pokey.

And phone calls—I got calls from all the big papers, and CBS, too. I was talking to a girl one night when my call waiting went off. I told her to hold on while I clicked over to see who it was. It was *The New York Times* calling, wanting to talk. I clicked back over to her and told her who was calling, and her comment was "you're kidding" and I said "Nope, I have to go talk to *The New York Times*."

Then one night in late June, I answered the phone and it was my delegate coordinator calling for the Clinton campaign to see if there was anything they could do for me.

I said, "No, but I can sure do something for you." I told him about myself, and that I was probably the most unusual delegate going to NYC. I told him about my interview, and sent him a copy of the interview on tape.

Three days later he called back. "Working Man, we saw your tape and we all love you here in Little Rock. I sent the tape on to the group handling the convention, and there is a chance they might want to use you as part of the convention. We'll know if they want you in it next week. Call and check in every other day or so, and if anything breaks, I'll call you."

This was thrilling news to me, because anything that put me in the spotlight also put my quest towards being a voice for the workers in the spotlight there, also. I knew that if any disinterested party looked at my newspaper clippings and interview, they would see the potential there and want the Working Man to be a big part of the campaign.

It was the Fourth of July weekend, and Elesha and I had spent our annual vacation in Panama City, Florida. We had driven the 312 miles home that Friday and pulled up in the yard. I went to open the door, and when I did, I heard the phone ringing.

It was Little Rock calling. The Clinton aide had heard from the media agency in Washington. They wanted to use me and needed a photo. I had to go to an express mail company that evening, mail a picture portfolio to Washington, and charge it to the Clinton for President Campaign.

The two women working got a real kick out of handling something being charged to the Clinton Campaign.

I had no idea what was in store, but I had begun to really enjoy this role in which I found myself. I had seven days to go before I left for New York, and the tension was mounting. Naturally, on Thursday, two days before I was to leave, I was laid off from my job. Even though it was only temporary, I sure didn't need it.

Meanwhile, I was doing all I could to become part of the campaign. Since I figured all along that being a regular working class American at the convention was a newsworthy event in itself, I called a Tuscaloosa TV station and arranged an interview with them. They wanted to do it there at #3 mine, my own little hole in the ground. I agreed, but I did worry about how it would go.

You see, pulling an eight-hour shift in the coal mines is not an easy thing. There are times when it's not so bad, but when it gets rough, it can be draining physically and mentally.

I was days away from the trip of a lifetime, and on Tuesday of that week—that would make it July 7th—I called my delegate coordinator in Little Rock to see if they were going to use me as part of the convention presentation.

Let me interject something here. From the time I got my first call from the Clinton people in Little Rock, I was dealt with in a most cordial manner by most of the people I talked to. And before the DNC was held, they had an 800 number so I could call and talk every day, and I did. I would go to work and then come home, talk to *The New York Times*, read my mail from influence groups of all types, then call the National Headquarters of the soon-to-be Democratic candidate for President where I would talk to people that dealt directly with the brain trust that is now running the country. When I sent them the tape of my interview, they told me I was the greatest. They twice asked the president of my UMW Local if he could get me off from work to come and work for the Clinton campaign. And after I was selected to be honored by the convention, everybody said they were proud to know me, and, "We love you in Little Rock."

I am telling you this because I was told by President Clinton's aides in Little Rock that I was part of the convention, and I would be a part of things after the DNC and the election. I was in daily communication with HQ Central, Little Rock, Arkansas—the nexus of the Clinton campaign—and these people who were the Clinton State Field Representatives were on a first-name basis with me and told me to call them to stay informed.

When I got to New York, I spent some time with my coordinator and he gave me my most prized campaign button, the coveted "I'm a FOB" button. That stands for "Friends of Bill," the Little Rock support group that was so important to his early primary successes. I even met with a bunch of them there in Madison Square Garden where we exchanged pleasantries, and I took several pictures of all of them gathered in front of the podium, before the security people chased us away. What I'm saying is that I was told by these agents of the Clinton camp that I was one of them. I was accepted by the Clinton staff as a factor in the election. They liked me. They said they loved me. I began to think I was a part of it all, and I began to act like it.

On that Tuesday night in July of 1992 when I was told I was going to be a prominent part of the Democratic Convention, I felt I was going to be able to get the kind of coverage needed to effectively convey that we the working people of this nation are going to be heard from, no matter what, no matter how long it takes. Again, I had a round of telephone calls to all my followers. By this time I had a regular group of people I called when there was a development. I told them to be sure and watch the convention, because I was going to be a part of it.

So, my departure date was drawing near. I had another TV interview coming up—filming me as I came off the elevator at work—and I was dirty and in my coal-mining attire.

As I mentioned earlier, I knew it was going to be tough doing anything well after eight hours of hard bull labor in the mine, but you have to deal with the media on their terms. I had to sparkle for the camera and try to be the astute and concise voice of the American worker, and I had to let the viewers know one of them was going into battle for them. It was to be a tough day at work, made tougher by the fact that I knew what was waiting for me when I came out.

I went in that day and pulled my eight hours. When I got on the elevator to come out that afternoon, I took a deep breath and did my best to compose myself. With a lurch, I headed up towards the light.

# CHAPTER 11

## A Blooper You'll Never See

As I reached the surface, I was not in a real hurry to get off the elevator. I could see the camera cranking away, making a tape of everyone as they got off the "cage," which is coal mine slang for the metal box (20 feet by 12 feet by 9 feet) that is used to carry men and supplies in and out of the mine. I walked off in a leisurely manner, doing my best to look heroic and determined. Try that wearing a dirty face and tremendously soiled, dirty, filthy, greasy overalls. I did the best I could, though, and one shot of me they used was quite satisfactory. I then went to get cleaned up and into my street clothes for the actual speaking part. While I was dressing, I thought about what I was going to say. I decided that I would wing it just like I had during my first interview a month earlier.

They had a regular newsman to interview me and provide the fill-in, and he had an assistant to help him in his filming and sound recording. And what an assistant. She was a very attractive woman, early twenties, dressed for a hot July afternoon in loose, comfortable clothing. Remember, as this is taking place I am a 42-year old man who spends all his time taking care of his daughter, with no social life or time for lady friends. I don't get out much, and being around young, beautiful women dressed in thin, summer clothing was something I was not in the habit of doing. In addition, I had just spent eight hard hours staring at coal, rocks, and other men, none of which could be described in terms of beauty, other than "in a stark contrast to" mode. What I'm saying is that she was a bit of a distraction, albeit a most pleasant one.

They set up the cameras and began the session. They were going to film for 20 minutes or so and cut it down to a seven-minute spot. I talked about my goal to be the voice of the working-class American at the convention. I spoke of how Clinton would rebuild the Party and sweep the election in November. The young lady's job was to stand directly in front of me, about twelve inches away, and hold the mike up to my face. Let me interject something here: I am not a sexist. I have a daughter, and I want her to have every opportunity in life. But this man-woman stuff transcends all boundaries, and she was a very impressive woman. I became distracted through no fault of my own.

I had done a good job of watching what I said, and we were moving towards the finish. Then I was asked if I thought this was a big election, and if I would be working during the campaign. I looked her in the eye and said, "Yes, I think this will be the biggest erection I've been involved with." My only excuse was my fatigue and her loveliness. I told her, "I knew I would be hard pressed to do this without being affected by you. You are a very pretty woman."

For my daughter's sake I'm glad it ended up on the cutting room floor. It would have made a great blooper for one of those shows, though. I concluded the interview and went home.

Later that day, I was anxiously awaiting the evening news to see what was used and what was not. Since it was short, I don't mind giving you a transcript of it. Seeing me in my work clothes and hearing me speak about being involved with the presidential election made for a highly contrasted interview, I think.

### TRANSCRIPT OF INTERVIEW OF JULY 10TH, 1992

News Anchorman: "Good evening. Tonight, we introduce you to J. R. Hammond, an area coal miner who's headed to the Democratic National Convention."

(Camera shot of a bunch of coal miners getting off the elevator, with lens finally coming to rest on yours truly)

Anchorman: "A total newcomer to the political scene is expected to make quite a splash. He is not a candidate, or party official, or campaign organizer; he's a coal miner turned first-time delegate from Woodstock, Alabama, and as our reporter says, he's very serious about this new role."

(Camera shot of coal miners, and then a shot of me, dirty face, dirty clothes and all)

Reporter: "In the heart of Alabama's coal country, a veteran coal miner says he's facing an extraordinary opportunity, a chance to help make history. J. R. Hammond, known to his coworkers as Hammer, has adopted a new name these days: the Working Man. He adopted this name after deciding to run as an Uncommitted delegate from Alabama to the Democratic National Convention. To the amazement of many, this man won."

Working Man: "It's a true case where an American worker, just an ordinary person, stepped forward and tried to take part and was able to carve out a piece of the action—to carve out a place to stand and make a stand."

Reporter: "Hammond says he's had few political ties in the last twelve years, but now that he's back involved, he wants to be the voice for a certain group of people: the average, everyday, blue-collar worker."

Working Man: "I ran because working people need a voice at the Democratic Convention. There'll be plenty of lawyers, plenty of politicians, and there'll be at least one working man.

Reporter: His coworkers say it's only fitting that Working Man travels to New York. Layoffs and hard times have become a way of life for many of their peers."

John Stewart (President UMWA District 20): "They've been put back in the closet. Working people, who are the taxpayers of this country, have been forgotten for the last twelve years. It's time for them to let us out of the closet."

Reporter: "Hammond says that time is now. Originally uncommitted, Working Man has quickly latched on to the Clinton campaign. He says the convention can be a crucial moment for the American worker."

Working Man: "This is the year the American workers come back to the Party. We will sweep in, in November."

Reporter: "So for a week, "Working Man" Hammond will replace his miner's outfit with clothes for the work to come: being the voice of the American worker."

I had to run a copy of this interview over to my good friend Michael Bolden and his lovely wife Laura, because they had missed it when it was broadcast. They were the last people I saw—outside of Elesha—before I left for New York.

It was awfully hard going to sleep that night. I faced an exciting challenge: to be the voice of the American worker at the Democratic National Convention. I was not going to be a wallflower at this dance. I was going to tell the country that we, the working people of this nation, are going to be a force to be reckoned with from now on. I was going to stand and be counted, to actually be among those playing a pivotal role in the Second American Revolution of 1992, to stand face to face with the soon-to-be President of this great and beautiful nation and say, "Hello there, I'm J. R. Hammond from Woodstock, Alabama."

Anyway, this ends part one of the book. Part two will be the trip to the DNC in NYC and all that entailed. See you there.

# 2

## Hope The Plane Don't Crash !!!

# CHAPTER 12

## Don't take a cab, because some people who have cabs are not cab drivers and they will take you off, rob you and kill you, not necessarily in that order

My mother, my daughter, and I made our way to Birmingham Municipal Airport that Saturday morning of July 11, 1992, in a buoyant mood. Elesha told me not to worry, that she and Granny would be just fine in my absence. I checked in my luggage, and went to the gate to wait. I kissed Elesha, hugged Mom, and then got on board the New York-bound sky trolley.

I had a seat in the extreme rear of the plane, back where the stewardesses prepare meals and such. I sat by myself for the first part of the flight, then was joined by a doctor when we made our stop in Cincinnati. He and his daughter were going to New York for a tennis tournament. He imparted to me the story of how his daughter was an up and coming tennis player, and she hoped to do well that week. It was a very pleasant flight.

We flew in to LaGuardia Airport across the harbor and by the Statue of Liberty. Of course, it really does give one a chill to see it for the first time.

People who don't travel much by air really don't understand the ease and convenience it gives one. I had flown before, but this was the best flight I had ever had. I suppose it was where I was going, what I was going to, and what I was going to do that made it so enjoyable.

We landed. As I made my way through the terminal, I became aware of all the goings-on about me. There were all kinds of people everywhere, a lot of nice suits, beautiful women, and the most unusual public announcement I have ever heard: "Attention, please,

*Waiting to board the plane to New York.*

those arriving for the Democratic National Convention are to ask those in blue DNC clothing for directions to their hotel shuttles. Do not take a cab because some people with cabs are not real cab drivers and will take you off and rob you and kill you."

I thought to myself that maybe I should get back on the plane now. But I walked on through the terminal, taking in the scenery. I was carrying a shoulder bag, a long suit bag, and a brief case I had borrowed for the occasion.

I made my way to the luggage pickup point where I waited for my other bags to show up. I tried to get interviewed by a reporter from NPR, but I suppose I was too average-looking to be part of their interview circle. Among the people in my crowd that are aware of NPR's existence, the initials stand for Nuts, Perverts, and Radicals. Where else can you hear a book review on the latest lesbian travel guide. But I like to listen, anyway.

My stuff finally showed up, and after I got my things together I headed for the area where the buses were waiting to carry us to the hotel assigned to each state. We stayed at the Loews Summit, which was one block from the Waldorf and 1¹/₂ blocks from where Arkansas people and the President-to-be were staying.

On the ride in, I checked out this largest of American cities. As I looked out the window, I thought to myself that I couldn't ever live in a place this congested and wondered if I would be able to make it for a week in this concrete jungle (I heard New York called this in some movie, and it sure seemed to fit).

I was all this time talking to those other delegates riding along with me. Evidently, the planes from Kansas, Kentucky, and my silver bird from Birmingham all came in at the same time because that's who was on the bus with me: people from Kansas, Kentucky, and me, from Alabama.

In a real sense, I was as alone as I've ever been when I arrived at the convention. There was no one even close to being like me there, and I for sure knew not a soul there. Blue-collar life has its rewards, its moments in the sun, and at times I would not trade it for anything, but political power, political clout, and political high ground aren't among them.

So, I looked at things from a totally different perspective than every other delegate there—from the ground floor, looking up at those above me running the country, and not having any power to affect the outcome of events as they unfolded in my life. See, as I told you before, I am just like most of you, being pulled along for the ride and hoping the plane doesn't crash.

The first real difference between myself and the other delegates appeared on the bus ride. I am a friendly person and spoke freely to everyone I ran across involved with the DNC. This included all those on the bus heading into the hotel district with me. We talked about them, we talked about me, and when I told them I was a poet, I was forced to recite to the whole bus two of my better works: "Ode to a Second Divorce," and "Little Big Horn Revisited." (I'll do them later for you as they came up again one night at the hotel.)

Anyway, we were rockin' along having a big ol' time, with their swapping DNC stories and them listening to my poetry. I asked them if they were new at this, also, but everyone had been to Atlanta in '88 and/or San Francisco in '84.

Then we began talking politics. Most of the other people on the bus with me were women, for some reason, and we talked a good bit

J. R. HAMMOND

on women's issues. Being raised by my mother and grandmother—and raising a daughter myself—has made me a real champion of women, and I am in the corner of the fairer sex, believe you me. I am also a fool for a pretty face. Then, this lady delegate from Kansas asked me about the '88 election, and what role I played in the campaign in Alabama. I told her the same role I played in the '84 campaign, none.

This did raise some eyebrows, and led to a discussion of issues and to my telling her that not only had I not played a role in the campaign, I didn't even vote for Mondale or Dukakis.

Boy, did I ruffle some of their feathers when I said that. She looked at me and asked how could I be a Democrat and vote for Reagan and Bush?

I stated I did not say I voted for them, for in fact I did not vote for anyone for President in '84 or '88. Other people joined in then, saying that not voting for was the same as voting against, and I heard someone say "traitor" in the background. I then stopped what I was doing and told them something that was later to illustrate the key reason why Bill Clinton is President today.

When one of them called me a traitor, that really got to me and sparked my fire.

I told them this: "I am a working person that is not involved in politics in any way despite the fact that I am riding on this bus here with you, going to my hotel here in New York City for a six-day stay so that I can attend the Democratic National Convention as a delegate from Alabama's 7th Congressional District. I am the type person that has not voted for a Democratic candidate for President since 1980. I am working-class America. Now I was born and raised a Democrat; I vote Democratic in every election and, if asked, tell people I am a Democrat. I thought FDR and the sun in the sky were the two things that kept this country going during the Great Depression. I supported Johnson, Humphrey, Carter, and even McGovern.

"But if I, a born, raised, diehard and in-my-blood Democrat could not bring myself to vote for the Democratic nominee, then how in the world could we expect the voter with no affiliation to vote for us? If a person like myself—who had never voted Republican in my life—couldn't bring myself to vote for the Party nominee, how could we think the man on the street could be for us? We couldn't. That's why we keep losing. That's why I got involved in the first place, and why I am here in New York City: to try and get the Party back where it needs to be—where we can win for a change."

This little tirade silenced my critics and I settled back to look around and shut up for a while. When we got close to my hotel, I looked out and saw a prostitute asleep on the sidewalk lying up against a building.

I don't think she was a regular homeless person because of the way she was dressed. I could have been wrong, though. Maybe there are a lot of young attractive homeless women wearing satin hot pants and halter tops up there, but I just didn't see them. I saw this one, anyway, and all the ladies on the bus let out a gasp and an "Ohh, look at that" as we drove past.

I reached my hotel. They had a very good system for getting people and their rooms together, and in no time I was on the fourth floor, unpacking and calling home to tell them I had arrived. New York, I am here, so show me what you have to offer—as long as it's not too expensive. And I mean Alabama expensive, not New York expensive. There is a difference.

We were given a cardboard suitcase full of little knickknacks, pins, a DNC-New York-'92 key chain, and best of all, an official DNC '92 badge that said "Democratic National Convention Delegate." I wear it on my baseball cap to this day. I made sure everything was put away, and I headed out to see what was shaking in the Big Apple.

# CHAPTER 13

## Hey Mister, You Wanta Buy a Rolex, Cheap?

I left my room and headed down the hall towards the elevators. It was about 4 p.m. and I really hadn't eaten anything all day, so I felt this was first on my New York agenda. You know when you're going to be somewhere for a week and you have a very limited budget to work with, the word "economy" takes on a new meaning. Part of the delegate material given to us included a restaurant guide that listed each place by its reputation for good food and its price range. And believe you me, never in my life could I imagine myself paying for a meal what some of these places charged. There was all kinds of material to peruse in my spare time, and I thought it would be wise to know as much as I could about what all was going on. This later turned out to be of more importance than I could have thought that first day in New York.

I hit the sidewalks (I bet I walked more places than any other delegate) of New York for the first time. As luck would have it, I found a very nice Chinese place only two blocks away. The food was hot, tasteful, and only twice what I would have normally paid in Alabama. My first meal in New York was beef, broccoli, and rice. I finished up and decided to walk around some more because it didn't cost anything, and it was a lovely day for a walk.

I tried not to look too much like a tourist, but hey, when you see a guy wearing a dozen campaign buttons and you know there's a convention in town, it wasn't hard to figure out that I was not from around there. There is a big police precinct headquarters just across the street from the Loews, so I went over to say "Hi" to some of New York's Finest, get the low-down about what part of town it was safe to find one's self in, and even more importantly, what part of town it was not safe to find one's self in.

I don't know if the New York police are like that all the time, but

I would like to take the time now to say that never in my life have I been treated with such courtesy and patience. These people in blue that I spoke to were on their best behavior, of that I'm sure. But you can't make a genuinely friendly attitude appear and disappear at will, and those guys in the NYPD station across the street from the Loew's Summit were no less than heroically friendly. And I got the scoop from them, big time. They told me to use common sense, and whatever I did, not to buy any watches, because you can't get a Rolex for $10—even in the Big Apple. After a very pleasant conversation with several officers, and my fear of being attacked and killed in broad daylight allayed, I took off on a Saturday afternoon stroll through Manhattan.

You hear how cold and indifferent the people are supposed to be up there—and I did meet one or two with an attitude problem—but hey, I walked along and said "hello" to people. Those that spoke English spoke back to me and were very friendly. And since the homeless and street-types had been moved away from the down-town area, I encountered no one who asked for money. It would have done them no good to ask, anyway, since I was—for all practical purposes—as broke as they were.

My room had a small refrigerator, so I decided to find a grocery store and buy some soft drinks so I wouldn't have to pay $1.00 for a canned Coke. I got directions from the police to an A&P store, and it was, without a doubt, the weirdest grocery store I have ever been in. I realize space is really at a premium there in NYC, but until I entered that store I didn't realize how they could get a full-sized market into the space of a single-family house. They can't go long-ways or sideways in the search for shelf space, so they stack goods up to the sky, fill every available spot with something for sale, and put some in places where there was no available space.

Also, they don't have quite the same foodstuffs on the shelves there in NYC that we have here in Heartland Alabama. I decided a couple of big bottles of Mountain Dew would tide me over for a day or two, and I put a bag of chips in my basket to keep the drinks company. Did I mention I had figured out before I left home one way to hold my sustenance bill in check? As you know, we Southern-ers are partial to barbecued pork sandwiches, so I had a pound chopped specially just for me by the local B-B-Q emporium. I wrapped it in plastic and froze it the night before I left. It survived the trip nicely and had found a temporary home in the fridge in my room. The last item to go in my shopping cart was a package of buns so that I would at least have a good ol' Alabama hickory-smoked flatnose sandwich to chow down on if bad came to worse.

While in line to pay for my groceries, I got into a conversation with a man from Scotland who now lived in our fair nation. He seemed like a real nice guy, and I hope he has a good life over here. He had a great accent. Funny thing is, he thought I had one, too. A Southern drawl must not be too common in Scotland.

Back at the hotel, I put away my grocery bill in the nice little icebox. As I looked out my fourth floor window at the lengthening shadows, I realized I was in New York City on a Saturday night. I was single, of age, and had no reason not to go out—if you'll pardon the expression—and raise a little hell.

But I did, really, have a reason not to go out and kick up a little dust. I actually had two hundred million reasons not to go out and do something wild and crazy. You, blue-collar America. I am sure you have heard people all your life tell you they were representing you in some fashion or another. But how many of these people were actually like you, lived the life you live, and were able to relate to you as something more than the electorate that had to be dealt with every so often? I can tell you the answer: none of them.

I have spent my whole life in the company of working-class people. I am a working-class person myself with twenty years of experience. So when I was elected under the name "Working Man" Hammond, I made a vow that I would carry myself in a manner that would not bring any dishonor to those I was standing up for there in NYC. I would not let you down by being anything less than what you would expect from the only one of you ever elected to this job. So, despite the fact that the Big Apple lay right outside my door, I did not go out on the prowl and get wild.

Around 10 o'clock, I did decide to go out for a stroll. As I turned to walk up the street towards the Waldorf Astoria, I looked down the fantastic panorama that is Lexington Avenue on a Saturday night. Wow! I could see why this town is the cultural center of America. There were things going on everywhere, and I was right in the midst of it. I probably looked more like a tourist at this moment than I ever had in my life. So, I suppose it was my out-of-town look that prompted the tap on the shoulder I received shortly thereafter.

As I turned to face the individual that had come up to me, I saw a young black man—say, early twenties—standing there. He motioned for me to move out of the middle of the sidewalk and follow him over to a quiet alcove. He looked both ways and said in a low voice, "Hey mister, you wanta buy a Rolex, cheap?" I had read it in the paper before I left Alabama, had been warned earlier that day by the cops at the station, and here I was being asked the most famous con game question ever. I envisioned Jethro Bodine of the old "Beverly Hillbillies" television show when he bought the Hollywood Bowl and the Los Angeles freeway. I could not help but laugh in this guy's face. I told him, "Thanks but no thanks, I have five of them back home, don't care what time it is anyway, and would you like to buy a two carat diamond ring—real cheap?" I don't think he got the joke.

I walked around for about an hour until I headed back to turn in. Down a side street, I noticed a man wearing one of those styrofoam straw hats you see during election campaigns, and he motioned for me to come down to where he was. I walked down there to see what was going on, and when I got close, I saw he was a barker for an all-nude bar.

Not having been in one, I did have some curiosity about it. I asked him what the deal was. A charge of $10 entitled you to: watch the show, three beers, and a souvenir mug. Ten dollars was about my budget for the night. Since I hadn't spent any of it—and after a very long day I was really in need of some kind of stress relief—I went in to have a beer and get that mug.

They had some very lovely and talented women working there, and as I was finishing my last beer one of them named Angel came up and sat down next to me.

She said "hello," and at the same time the bartender lady said, "Why not buy the lady a drink?"

I asked her if she wanted a drink, and she said, "Yes, please buy me a frozen daiquiri."

The barkeep said "okay" and was just going to make her one when I said, "Wait a minute, how much?"

The dancing girl and the barkeep both looked away, and the bartender said in a low voice, "$37."

I hurt my chin when my mouth dropped open. "No ma'am, I can't go that route." I looked back to where the dancer had been sitting, and she was making tracks to greener pastures.

I decided to leave then before I got in any trouble I couldn't get out of. But one thing still remained to be done. I asked the drink-slinger where my mug was. She looked incredulous and said, "You want the mug?"

I suppose most of the clientele were more interested in other aspects of the club's atmosphere and darn few mugs were given out there. It was made out of high-grade plastic and keeps beverages cold. I got out of there quickly, mug in hand, and made my way back to the fourth floor of my temporary New York domicile.

I lay back in my bed and wondered how many suckers bought those $40 drinks without asking the price? No doubt, 99 out of 100 got stuck for a bar tab equal to the price of their daily hotel bill. Thank goodness I had the presence of mind not to buy something without asking what it cost.

I was suddenly very tired, and so around 1 a.m. I killed the light and called it a day.

I had traveled a thousand miles, got settled in, developed a real feel for the city, had not been suckered in on a watch deal, and escaped from that bar without getting stuck for a $40 drink. I was ready to be the voice of the American worker there at the convention, and since I had a big day coming up, I closed my eyes and fell fast asleep.

It took little time, believe you me.

# CHAPTER 14

## In which I make two absolutely smashing parties, become somewhat acquainted, meet a lovely art history major, and decide some art is not necessarily art

S unday morning sunlight was filtering into the room, and boy, did I have a lot to do that day. I was to be interviewed by an AP reporter that morning, and I wanted to be in my best and most personable frame of mind when I had my shot at this media representative. I knew one thing right away: that myself and food had become strangers and breakfast at that moment seemed to be one of the most beautiful words in the English language.

The reporter chose that moment to call. He was to meet me in the lobby at 9 a.m., so I had one hour to get some groceries into my stomach. I showered, shaved, and went through the usual morning grooming procedures. I wanted, of course, to look my best, so I did my darnedest to get presentable. Luckily, my best is not at the upper end of the beauty scale, and I was able to get it all done by 8:45. I headed down to the front desk to see if the reporter had arrived.

Each delegate from Alabama was given a packet of invites to functions planned and paid for by Friends of Alabama Democrats. We had four official parties to attend, and I had lost track of where all I was supposed to be and at what time. As luck would have it, my arrival at the front desk coincided with the arrival of two beautiful women who were talking to the desk person as I walked up. They were asking him about the breakfast being thrown for the Alabama delegation up in the Penthouse Club Room. It hit me I was supposed to be there already, and I quickly followed them both to the elevator. I spoke with them on the way up, and they were from Georgia, had friends in Alabama, and were invited to attend—so here they were.

As we reached the 17th floor, I must admit I was a bit nervous about the imminent encounter with the rest of the Alabama delegation. After all, I had been around some of these people for 30 minutes—five weeks earlier—and had never been around the rest of them. But I was bound and determined not to be in awe of them or intimidated by them. After all, I represented more people than anyone in the Alabama delegation and, indeed—as I stated every time anyone asked me—more people than anybody at the convention because I represented working-class America.

I followed them around and when I looked at the room we were in, the Penthouse Club Room, I could see that this trip to the Big Apple was going to be even more than I thought it would be. For the first time in my life I was going to see how the other half lives.

There were people all around eating, talking, walking, and just having a most enjoyable time. There was a whole wall filled with a huge buffet of every kind of brunch edible known to man. The aroma of all that fabulous food was overpowering. And there were four—count them, four—chefs cooking omelettes for those lucky enough to be there. Boy, it was heaven for a man with an empty stomach. I was actually stunned by the array, but I found enough composure not to act like it. I got in the serving line, and casually strolled along looking at foodstuffs that, had I not made this trip, I know I probably never would have had the privilege to see. Then I reached a chef who asked me what I wanted in my omelette. I told her to surprise me.

Since I had gotten there late, all the good tables were taken and I had to go outside on the terrace to eat. I started to eat while taking the time to look around. When that first bit hit my tongue, I got culinary sensory overload. Words cannot convey how superior to any eggs I had ever eaten this masterpiece was. It was amazing. I ate the rest of it and looked around the city.

The overall setting drove home the realization that the elite live differently from the rest of us. They don't just live better by having all the bills paid; they exist on a higher level of excellence. This was the best food I had ever eaten, and I was eating it on the penthouse terrace 17 stories into the New York sky. The sun was in my face, and a fresh breeze blew gently around me as I looked out on a magnificent New York skyline. I wasn't in Kansas any more, Toto.

There were speeches and introductions, and we were told the plans for the party that night at the Whitney Museum of American Art. If breakfast was this good, dinner at the museum could very well be fatal. I had just finished my second omelette when the reporter arrived. He took some photos of me—most heroic-looking, I might add—with a backdrop of the New York skyline, and afterwards he had a bite to eat as well. We headed off for a subway ride down to Macy's so's I could get my daughter a souvenir from the big "M."

You hear about all the violence that goes on in the subway, and I'm sure it isn't always as safe as it was that Sunday morning. I work underground so I am used to subterranean rail travel and was not impressed by the actual subway cars themselves. I did enjoy being part of a Sunday morning subway crowd, though, and I must admit the multilevel format had me the least bit bewitched. Still, I had a guide so we made it to Macy's posthaste.

After I had gotten my everpresent yet 1,000-mile-away daughter Elesha a Macy's souvenir tote bag, my guide and I walked around and checked out the downtown area some. It was very neat, both in an actual physical sense and in the fact it was flattering to walk around and have someone write down what you say and how you feel about things. It had to end, so, after I had him go over instructions on how to take the subway back to my hotel, I was on my own in downtown NYC.

Of course I got lost and ended up—I know not where—wandering around and asking people how to get back to my temporary residence. Everybody I talked to while I was wandering around that Sunday was as nice and friendly as you could hope for. It was refreshing to meet people in another part of the country and have them act towards me like I act towards travelers I encounter in my Woodstock, Alabama, homeland. And I always try to leave a good impression with those just passing through. After all, it's not like I'm going to have to put up with them after they leave.

I had somewhat of a problem getting good directions because a good many of the folks I was meeting were from out of town also. I remembered there was a celebrity diner down the block, and I finally got headed back in the general direction of my room.

My room, by the way, was not the big suite you often see pictured in movies and such.

It was smaller than any motel room I had ever had, and it was very plain, to boot. As working-class America is used to doing, I had to get the cheapest and was glad to get that. It had a wall safe, a very nice shower, and cable television. Anyway, I only slept there because every waking moment I was somewhere doing something. I must

J. R. HAMMOND

say the bed was most comfortable (what little time I was on it).

By now it was the middle of the afternoon, and we were leaving for the museum on a special bus around 7 p.m. I got ready early and went downstairs to the lobby. I hung around the hotel lobby a good bit because there were new people coming in all the time, and many were of the female persuasion. I can't see why you should talk politics to a man when you can talk politics to a woman just as easily. It's just not in my nature to associate with men when I can associate with women on an equal basis. At the time, I was single and 100 percent U.S. male.

Personally, I have a real problem with political correctness. Some things have been carried too far by those that are not of the working class. People that work together get along. We have to. When you're waist deep in a pile of coal slurry (a jell-like mixture of coal and water) you don't care who it is that will help you out of it. And all American working people have one thing in common: We don't like people who are too sorry to work. I'm not referring to the disabled, those unable to find work, or retired people. I'm talking about those folks in good health that are just too lazy to get off their behinds and go get a job.

Enough of this soapboxing for now. I am not writing this to just tell the world how I feel about things. I am writing this to tell you the story of an average American guy's accidental election as delegate to the 1992 DNC. I am writing this so that perhaps other working-class Americans like myself will become inspired and make the effort to make this a better country for those of us that do every dad-blame bit of work in America. I am writing this because I had the opportunity. If I don't write it, others will never know what it was like to be part of American politics at a high level.

I was meeting people from all over this nation—mainly from Alabama, North Carolina, and Kansas—as all three state delegations were holed up there at the Loews with me. I met some really fine people from Kansas (especially a 22-year-old coed from Kansas University who was just a doll). And the North Carolina folk were the most hospitable people I've ever met. I plan to go visit the Tarheel state someday. Maybe I'll see some of my friends there.

Eventually, the buses were ready, so off I went—along with all the other Alabamians and their guests—to the Whitney Museum of American Art. The building that houses the museum is very impressive, very artsy, with a most flowing design. I was impressed with the inside, also. We were assigned a tour guide, a rather charming and beautiful woman in her mid-twenties, who seemed very at home showing us around. Talk about a work of art!

We first went up to the third floor where the modern art was on exhibition. As the elevator doors opened, my eyes fell upon a metal box full of big white rocks. It wasn't a solid box, more like a metal framework, where you could see this wonder of nature—a bunch of rocks in all their splendor.

The guide then took several minutes telling us how the artist had seen these rocks at the rock place and had a vision. He would, by putting these rocks in this metal box, convey the message that his vision of natural art contained. She told us all the trouble he went to (I think she said it was a male artist, as some of those rocks were pretty big for a woman to be handling) having those particular rocks sent there and then restacked in just the position he had found them in. There was a moment of silence after she had finished, and, being an expert in all kinds of rock, I began to tell my impression of this particular exhibit.

"Well, let me tell you what I think of this. If a person were to spend all their time in an office, away from the actual world as it is seen in nature, and if this person never actually got out of their apartment and had not actually seen a pile of big rocks anywhere in their adult life, then these people might consider this to be art. However, I work in an underground coal mine and I see more rocks every day than I care to tell about. I have seen how mother nature actually stacks big rocks (as roof falls are numerous in a coal mine). In other words, I work with this kind of thing every day, and we in the mines throw away stuff like this because it won't burn and you can't sell it. We dig out rock and coal and throw the rock away. In fact, I sit on rocks just like these and eat my lunch sometimes. I prefer not to, but it beats eating standing up. Like I said, if you never experience nature, maybe this is impressive. But it looks like a good place to eat lunch to me."

And of course, my quote made the papers in Birmingham. Not the good stuff about how those nature-starved individuals had reason to call this box of rocks "art," but the part about how we mine the coal and throw away the rocks—and especially how I sit on rocks like those to eat my lunch. By the way, if you can find something softer, don't sit on a rock. Most of them are hard, and they can be sharp and cut you. I sit on them only as a last resort.

J. R. HAMMOND

Next, the guide showed us over to a big wall canvas with a 3-D effect. As I was looking closer, it seemed to me for all the world that someone had taken a bunch of garbage, including a fish skeleton, laid it on a canvas and painted over it. And perched on top of the painting—as though it was lording over the whole thing—was a stuffed chicken.

At that moment, the guide began to tell us about how the artist wanted to convey a message of a ruined environment. He had actually laid a bunch of garbage on a canvas and painted over it. Well, I thought if a bunch of garbage is what the artist was trying to convey, he certainly hit the mark. I tried not to, but I could not help but laugh out loud at this thought. The guide then looked at me for comment. "Well, I really like the chicken." She pulled back slightly and in a most aggravated voice said, "It's not a chicken, it's a pheasant!" "Oh, yes," I said, "I can see where that would make a difference." I lost interest in further aspects of this museum's third floor and decided to strike out on my own.

I went down to the second floor where there was a really fabulous exhibit of works by the great American artist, George Bellows. He painted scenes of ordinary American life from a man's perspective. At least, that is what his paintings said to me. There were some beautiful still life depictions, like softened snapshots, showing superb scenes of seasonal celebration. (Alliteration, thy name is Working Man.) But to my male eyes the scenes he portrayed from boxing matches—club fights mostly—were eerily compelling. As I looked at his works I turned a corner and ran into, literally, Alabama's 5th Congressional District Representative, the Honorable Bud Cramer. I introduced myself, and he said he had heard of me. I said I had heard of him, too, and he told me to call him Bud. He seems to be a really nice individual, a great leader, and since he didn't care much for the garbage painting, either, he is a good judge of art.

We explored the second floor for a while longer, pausing to look at a table full of books. I reached for one of the books to see what kind of reading material they had left lying around for us to look at when this guard came running up and told me "Stop! That's a piece of art!" After that I was nearly afraid to punch the elevator button to get the heck off the floors that contained art. I wanted to get down to the basement floor where the party was going on—and more importantly, food was being served (remember, my meal money was in finite supply, and I still had five more days to go).

If I thought the breakfast was amazing, then this party bordered on the metaphysical. If you're lucky enough to have money, don't bother to read this part because it will bore you. But if you are one of the tens of millions who have never hung out with the upper crust, then read on.

When I got off the elevator, I saw there was a group of around 75 to 100 people milling around in cocktail dresses and evening wear. I was certainly glad I had the foresight to wear my funeral suit. Clothes are not high on my list of priorities, and I only have one suit I bought to wear to my late stepfather's funeral. I don't wear it much, but I brought it along mainly for this affair. Boy, were those in attendance dressed to the nines. And there were waiters, umm, butlers, no, wait, uhhh, men and women dressed in tuxedos carrying around trays of food and passing them out to the guests as they would stand around and talk art, politics, and I suppose how much fun it is to have money. And they handed you glasses of champagne, and wine, and if you couldn't wait for them to bring it back you could go out to the patio area where there was a bar dishing out what you wanted when you wanted it.

The food on the trays was not beanie weenies or hot dogs, but rather those kinds of foods you see being served in the movies. There were (and I hope I spell it correctly) hors d'oeuvres of all types, roast beef on toothpicks, and—the most delicious of all—fried oysters served on little skewers with a most delicate mustard sauce. I must admit I was impressed. And these men and women carrying around these trays of delicacies were pleasant, gracious, and acted like they really cared about what they were doing. They were working people, too.

After meeting our millionaire host and some of his millionaire buddies, I mingled, chatted, and in general was a perfect guest by not causing any problems. Then, the guide who had shown us the third floor evidently had finished her last tour and joined us. As I mentioned earlier, I just naturally gravitate towards beautiful women, and I joined her for a spirited discussion of art. We discussed many things: artistic motivation, what the artist is trying to convey, if she had a steady boyfriend, and if she already had plans for after the party. Turned out she did, so I politely disengaged from the conversation and left her alone.

I had figured as much, but it never hurts to ask. When done in a benign manner, it is entirely proper to ask a member of the opposite

J. R. Hammond

*Enjoying new friends in New York.*

sex if they're interested in further negotiations. Alas, this was my one chance at personal art instruction by a trained professional (she had a degree in art history) and she had a prior commitment—story of my life.

One last note about the party: it seemed like no matter where I stood, by the time the trays of goodies arrived they were either empty or nearly so. Since I had already spoken to everybody rich and powerful and had struck out with the art history major, I decided something. Most everybody else there evidently attended parties like this on a regular basis, and since I couldn't get the girl, I was going to at least get some of the food. So, I followed one of the waiters back to where they were bringing the food from. At least I had first crack at the trays as they were being brought from the kitchen. I made it count.

Don't think from all this talk about food that I have some kind of fixation on it. I don't. But here I was at a party the likes of which I may never see again. I had absolutely nothing in common with almost everyone there, save being from Alabama. I was surrounded by people who never have to worry about paying the rent, or if their boss will get on their case that day at work, or if they will even have a job that day. Things that the working people of this country deal with every day seldom if ever cross these peoples' minds. Personally, I was laid off from work at the time and wasn't sure how I was going to pay July's house note. There was no way I could match any of these people (save my masculine skill and prowess) in most aspects of life. But by gosh, at that party I was on an equal footing for the food. The rest of the elite could have what I left them on the trays. It was a minute victory, but in the middle-class, blue-collar world that's the kind of victory we often have to settle for—insignificant and irrelevant.

Boy, were those good oysters.

Things wrapped up and we boarded the buses for our return to our hotel. We—all the delegates from all 50 states, plus the American territories—were also invited to a big party in Central Park that night, but our own party had run too long so we missed it. Despite the lateness of the hour, I was not sleepy or hungry and I knew there were things going on somewhere out in that big city. I didn't want to go home. I wanted to do something really cool this last night in town before the DNC started for real. What to do, what to do.

The answer came to me on the bus on the way back. And, as impossible as it seems, despite the fact that I had done things, seen things, been places and been a part of situations that never in my wildest dreams had I thought I would ever get to be a part of, my night hadn't even started yet.

# CHAPTER 15

## Bruce Willis, Arnold Schwarzenegger and a smart-mouth Yankee boy

We were headed back to the hotel. Someone was talking to the bus driver, and we discovered that he drove a tour bus for a living. We asked him for a private tour, and although he was under orders to go straight back to the hotel, with a little persuasion of the green kind (mostly fives and tens) we were soon taking a rogue midnight bus tour.

He carried us up and down the streets, telling us of the shops where you had to have your credit approved before you could even go inside, stores where you could shop by appointment only, and stores that sold $200 handkerchiefs and $400 neckties. It sounded a little pricey to me, but I don't get out much. Then he took us by some night spots, and the last two he carried us by were the Hard Rock Cafe and the club just down the street, the Planet Hollywood Club (owned by Bruce Willis, Arnold Schwarzenegger, and Sylvester Stallone).

He said the latter was the hottest spot in town at the moment, and that about the only time to go without a reservation and try to get in was late on a Sunday night—and even then it was unlikely. The thought crossed my mind that something from those clubs would make my little Darlin' happy. She wanted things from cool places, and they both sounded really cool. The last thing the driver told us about the Planet Hollywood Club was that sometimes the owners were there; you could party in the vicinity of some famous people, and that's why the place was so hard to get into. We arrived back at the hotel, I told the driver how much I enjoyed it, and I got off the bus. When I got back to my hotel room, I quickly changed into something more comfortable.

What working man wouldn't?

I asked the woman at the desk where a good night spot was, and she suggested something called Tavern On The Green in Central

Park. I hailed a cab, and the driver held the microphone up so that I could talk into it and tell the dispatcher where I wanted to go. He then radioed back to the driver and communicated to him in his native tongue. As cumbersome as it sounds, in a flash I was headed to T.O.T.G.

When I got there, I was told it was a private party, and I wasn't invited. I got back into the cab and told the dispatcher to carry me to the Hard Rock Cafe. I walked in and looked around.

It is a multilevel affair with every kind of rock and roll memento you would care to see on the walls, along with photos of famous musician-types that had passed through there—just like I was doing. I headed for the gift shop to purchase some kind of a keepsake for my sweet daughter Elesha. I finally decided on a "Save The Earth—Hard Rock Cafe" tee-shirt in bold neon pink. (Elesha really liked it, too.)

I went out into the New York night, joining the ranks of those enjoying that fair summer evening under the Manhattan sky. I started to hail a cab and go back home, but I looked down the street and saw a big crowd outside a place a block away. Then I remembered the Planet Hollywood Club. What was that the bus driver said? The best time to get in was late on a Sunday night? It was after midnight already, so maybe this was the time to go. Since I had been told by the police it was safe to walk the streets in this area, I walked that way.

As I got closer, I could see the crowd waiting to go in and a group with cameras that just seemed to be hanging around. They had those crushed velvet ropes set up on both sides of the carpet that led into the building, and I noticed a man the size of a small mountain standing there as a combination bouncer/doorman. I was wearing my DNC colors already, sporting my tiger-striped University of Alabama baseball hat and wearing a chest full of political buttons (including my favorite, a small, Democratic Party donkey pin with a bright red, flashing strobe light for its eye; it does get attention in a dark room).

As I said before, I am a friendly type so I walked up to the guy and told him, "Hello. How are you doing? So this is the Planet Hollywood Club, huh? Looks like a nice place."

He looked at me with a most amused gleam in his eye and asked me where I was from and if I was up there for the DNC. I told him I sure was and how could he tell?

He laughed at this, and asked me if the "A" on my cap stood for Arkansas. I told him, "Oh, but no. It stood for Alabama. I'm from a place called Woodstock, Alabama, which is right outside Tuscaloosa, Alabama, home of the University of Alabama Mighty Crimson Tide. They are winners of 10 football games in a row and are going to stretch that out to twenty-three games by January 1st of 1993. We are going to be undefeated this year and become national champions." He smiled broadly when I told him this, and said yes, he saw us destroy Colorado the year before and had bet on Alabama in that game.

We talked football for a while, and seeing that there were so many people in line ahead of me to get in, I decided to call it a night. I didn't feel like waiting who knows how long to get into the place. I told him I'd better be going, that it was nice to talk to him, and he should bet on us every game this next season.

He said, "Wait a minute. Don't you want to go inside? It's really neat."

I told him I did, but I didn't have the time to wait. He said, "Look, you don't want to eat dinner, do you? Come on in, be my guest."

With this, he unlocked the part of the rope that served as a gate at the end of the red carpet going into the entrance. I looked at the long line waiting to go in, motioned my head in their direction and said in a low voice, "What about them?"

He just smiled and said back to me, "I decide who goes in and who doesn't. Go ahead, be my guest."

I shook his hand and in I went. Like I said earlier, it sure pays to be nice to folks you meet. Will Rogers was a brilliant man.

As I looked around, I was very impressed. I had seen all the press coverage when the place opened, but nothing prepared me for the real thing close-up and in person. All the movie stuff was there, and it was a real treat just to walk around. I decided that since they were so nice about it, despite my limited resources, I would spring for a drink.

I walked up to the bar, and this very lovely barmaid came over and asked me what I wanted to drink. I looked into her pretty face and said, "I don't know, Sugar, surprise me." This had worked so good at that morning's brunch that I decided to use it again.

As I waited for her to return, I looked around, and there on the bar was a glass case. I moved in for a closer look, and inside were the blade-fingered gloves Johnny Depp wore in *Edward Scissorhands*. How very cool, I thought. The bar-belle then returned with my drink, which turned out to be vodka. I said "cheers," and turned it up. She smiled approvingly, and we began to talk. I told her about myself, where I was from, and why I was there in New York (Voice of the American worker, etc.).

We had a good talk, and she would come back to chat, after giving someone else a drink down at the other end of the bar. She told me all about herself, and yes, she was sorry but she had a steady boyfriend, but she was very flattered at my marriage proposal anyway. I may have had another drink while we talked, or two. She did warm up to me (she was one of those with good taste in people) and after a few more minutes, she leaned over the bar and said, "Do you like Bruce Willis?"

I said "Well, sure. All coal miners like Bruce Willis. He's a real man's man. I know he's your boss. Why do you ask?" She pointed back over my shoulder and said, "He's sitting right over there. He's a real nice guy. Why don't you go over and say hello? He would be glad to give you an autograph, too."

Well, now, I thought, I'll just do that. I got a cocktail napkin and borrowed her drink-order-taking pen and headed that way. The area where the tables were located was less well lit than in the bar, so I had to wait a minute for my eyes to adjust before I could try and find him. Then I saw somebody wearing a tee-shirt, tennis shoes, and cutoff jeans sitting in a most relaxed position with his legs extended, feet crossed at the ankles, and his hands behind his head. This had to be him, nobody else would go to this place dressed like that except the king of cool, Bruce Willis. I walked over.

Being my usual friendly self, I stuck out my hand and said, "Hello, Mr. Willis. I'm 'Working Man' Hammond from Woodstock, Alabama, up here for the DNC. I'm a coal miner, and all of us coal miners think *Die Hard* was great. Could I have your autograph for my daughter, Elesha?" As he shook my hand, he said, "Sure, pal, anytime." I watched him sign the paper, and then I thanked him again, which he acknowledged with a wink and a smile, and then I leaned over to pick it up.

As I did, I glanced over to my left, and two chairs down sat the old Terminator himself, Arnold Schwarzenegger.

Boy, I thought, when your luck runs good, it runs very good. I might as well get his while I'm this close. I took one step towards him and bodyguards appeared from nowhere, blocking my path. "Mr. Schwarzenegger is conducting business and cannot be disturbed."

I said "Sure thing, man," and backed away as gracefully as I could. "I'll just stand over here out of the way and watch." They both nodded in agreement, and I took up a position over in the aisle to the side and watched Arnold as he maintained a constant movement from table to table. He would go in the back of the place from time to time, where the tables were less visible, and stay there a minute or two and then come back to the main seating area.

I heard one of the other customers say the Kennedys were in the back. Since Arnold is married to one of them, it made sense. As I watched Bruce and Arnold relax in their club, I happened to look at the wall behind them, and once again this country boy was in for a surprise.

One solid wall of the club held this beautiful mural painting of the city of Hollywood as seen from a distance and from a high altitude. The big, famous "Hollywood" sign—so much a part of the city's lore—was clearly seen; there were miniature, electric lights in the windows of the buildings, and even the streetlights worked. I was so fascinated that for a minute or two I stared at the wall, taking in this bistro's work of art.

Now, there was a table about eight feet away from where I was standing with four people sitting at it. I, while not actually looking at the table and its occupants, was looking over it to view the mural. There were—from left to right—two gentlemen, a woman, and another man, all seated there.

While the first three people I mentioned were smiling and seemed to be having a good time, the last guy, who was the closest person to me and on my right, was sitting there all sulled up and not saying anything. I noticed the two guys on the right talking to each other and making pointing motions in my direction. Being the only guy in this dark club wearing a flashing, red, strobe light was definitely no way to keep a low profile.

Then, I noticed the two guys on the left motioning me over to their table. I'm not shy, so I strode over to see what they wanted. They wanted to talk. They asked who I was, where I was from, and questions about the DNC. I gave them what had become my standard reply: Woodstock, Mighty Crimson Tide, Voice of the American worker, and be sure and watch tonight because I was going to be on stage. They seemed to be genuinely interested in what I had to say, and even the woman was listening to me with a look of enjoyment on her face. All during this time, however, the guy on my right sat there with a look on his face like he was smelling a chicken house.

I was about ready to leave, so I told them how much I enjoyed talking to them and they replied in kind, and pleasantries abounded. I turned to leave, and I had a thought. I told them, "Hey, before I go, would you like to hear a good joke?" "Oh, yes," they replied, "Please tell us!" But before I could begin, the sulled-up guy that had been sitting there quietly suddenly looked up at me and said,

"Hey, why don't you **** off!"

The two guys that a second before had been smiling and joking with me suddenly got eyes as big as silver dollars. The woman dropped her face into her hand and was embarrassed beyond measure. The two guys looked at him, then back at me, at each other, and then looked at me again to see what I would do.

Me? I must admit I was at first surprised, then amazed, then all at once I was a coiled spring, and boy oh boy was I coiled. It was as though a red light started flashing in my mind, with each new flash saying "Danger! Danger! Danger! Danger!"

Both my freedom and this guy's face were in danger. This smart-mouth Yankee boy's nose was in danger of being damaged, and I was in danger of losing my freedom. Because unless something happened pretty quick, and I do mean quick, I was going to jail for assault and battery, and this smart-mouth Yankee boy was going to the emergency room. I was going to mess him up good. He was sitting in his chair—no doubt believing he was safe and secure—with his arms crossed, leaning back. He was a sitting duck. In a very short time I was going to show him my impersonation of a duck hunter on opening day of hunting season.

I was thinking, "Oh, great. It's the day before the DNC and I'm going to jail. What is this guy thinking? What's wrong with this creep, anyway? Does he think he can shoot his mouth off to anybody he wants, and it won't matter? Christ, I really hate doing this because of these other people. They were so nice, and on a Sunday night, too. Maybe they'll cut me some slack because I'm a delegate—I hope so.

I turned my body towards him and gave myself room to lean into it. I dropped my arms down to my side and made a fist with my right hand. I leaned over until my face was about 18 inches from his. "What did you say?" I asked, and got ready to swing. I had a spot on the left side of his nose already picked out. Just as I was about to tee off, the other two guys went into action.

Their hands shot out, and they both grabbed his arm at the same time. The one closest to me did the talking. "You tell this man you were just kidding now! Right now! I noticed both of them had a white-knuckle grip on his right arm. It must have hurt him enough to make him regain his senses to the point that he realized his mouth had put him in danger.

He looked at them, then looked at me, then looked straight ahead. He slowly lowered his eyes to where he was looking at the table. "Ah, I, ah, I was just kidding."

His friends looked up at me with the hope in their eyes that I would let him slide. I didn't want any trouble; I didn't start it, and I didn't want to cause these people any trouble. But I was going to make this guy be humble once in his life.

I got right in his face, and used my index finger to emphasize my words. "Okay, pal. I can take a joke as well as anybody. Now, if you'll tell me again you were just kidding, we'll shake hands like pals and forget it." He looked up at me, then back down at the table and said, "I was just kidding." I stuck out my hand and waited for him to shake it. He finally took hold of it in a weak grip, and I grabbed it forcefully and shook hands with gusto. I turned his hand loose and told the nice people at he table I was going. The spokesman said, "Wait! Tell us the joke!" I did, and drifted off towards the gift shop. I got Elesha a really nice, black "Planet Hollywood" tee-shirt that she wore at least once.

As I turned to go, I looked back towards their table, and the guy that did the talking gave me a wave. I thought for minute, then motioned for him to come over. When he did, I told him this:

"I have worked in the coal mines for twenty years. I'm not afraid of anything that walks, crawls, slithers along the ground, swims in the water or flies through the air. I spit on rocks and they fly apart. I face death every day on the job and don't care what happens to me. Now, you tell your friend this is the luckiest night of his life. I was in a good mood; I didn't want to upset Bruce and Arnold, but mainly, I really liked you guys and didn't want to mess up your Sunday night by making you spend it at a hospital trying to get your pal's face put back together. Also, I have other fish to fry. But tell him he owes you, because you saved his face and his ass tonight. Tell him how lucky he was."

"Oh, you can count on that. I'll tell him that more than once."

"Thanks." I said, "Don't mention it," and walked back out into the New York night. I spoke to the bouncer again, thanking him again and telling him about the rude, smart-mouth Yankee boy inside that I nearly had to civilize. He wanted to go back in, throw them out, and give their table to me, but I told him, "No, I have to be going, but thanks anyway." I reminded him to "bet on Alabama because we have a monster team this year." He hailed me a cab, and as I waved at him out the window while pulling away, he yelled "Roll Tide!" It was a fitting farewell.

I'm not a violent man. I normally have a long fuse on my temper, and most irritants flow off me like water off a duck's back. But that guy was just too smug, too smart-mouthed, and too sure he could say what he wanted to with impunity.

An interesting follow-up to this story came out six months later. A scientist issued a report on Southern men. According to him, Southern men will fist fight over verbal insults that the rest of the country pays no attention to. Seems that we are descended from Scottish hog farmers and have carried this code of chivalry down through the years. I called a talk radio show about this and said, "If I ever meet this joker, I'll whip his butt." That was a joke. But the scientist's theory sure explained why that guy just sat there like I wasn't going to do anything to his smart-mouth, Yankee boy behind. I came close to stomping his tail so flat he'd look like a beaver. I just made that expression up. I am a writer, you know.

I got home to my hotel without further trouble. As I was lying in bed, I noticed it was 2:30 a.m. It was the earliest I was to go to bed for the next six days. The DNC hadn't even started, and I had already had a Sunday that was a full 24 hours of adventure, and I now knew U.S. congressmen, U.S. senators, rich people, and Bruce Willis (slightly, anyway). I had nearly gotten in a fight in the hottest night spot in New York, and I had backed down a S.M.Y.B. in front of his friends. I was friends with the doorman at the Planet Hollywood Club and had purchased two great gifts for Elesha. I was ready for the DNC. Next stop, politics of the first magnitude: the 1992 Democratic National Convention.

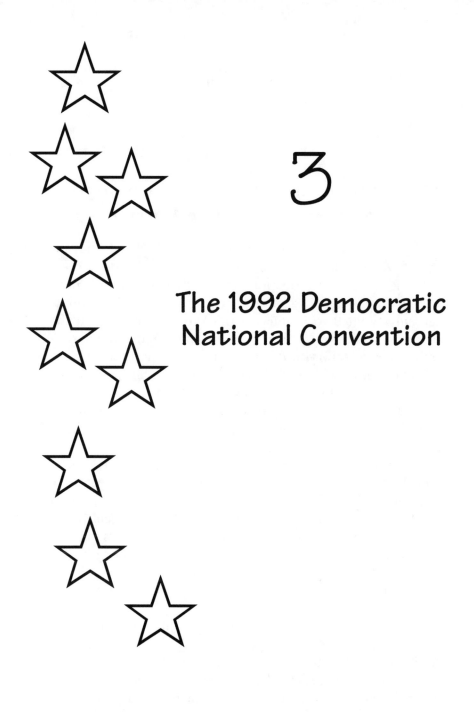

# 3

## The 1992 Democratic National Convention

# CHAPTER 16

## If the 'Star Spangled Banner' don't make you cry you don't really love America

When I awoke Monday morning, I felt fit and ready for the task before me of being a voice for working-class, blue-collar America. I showered and shaved with much gusto and energy. We had our first credentials meeting that morning, and I wanted to be there early. We met everyday in the penthouse banquet room, high atop the hotel. And, more importantly, somebody always had a breakfast spread waiting on us. Have you noticed how good free food tastes? This was being prepared by gourmet chefs, so it was magnificent in taste and appearance.

It was here that morning that I met the rest of the Alabama delegation and actually became friends with them (a couple of them, anyway).

We sat in our chairs and when the head of the Alabama Democratic Party called out your name, you went up and got your incredibly cool, holographic, 1992 DNC credentials that got you into the Garden and down on the convention floor. It seemed that most everyone was a bit standoffish, but, then again, I was the only delegate that didn't know anybody in the Democratic Party when I got elected. I was a total stranger to everyone, and as they say in the movies, I had to prove myself worthy before they would want to get to know me better.

I met a real labor leader that morning, Mr. Jim Allbright, who is now the Alabama president of the AFL-CIO. He told me he had a meeting to go to at the Downtown Sheraton that morning, so I thought I'd go along because the president of my own UMWA, Mr. Richard Trumka, was also supposed to be there. I made the passage from the Loews to the Sheraton, and lo and behold, I found myself sitting next to Mr. Trumka. I introduced myself, and we spoke for several minutes. He has been a good leader for the union, although I don't think he realized the significance of a rank-and-file coal miner being elected delegate. When he reads this book, I think he will.

I had spoken to my delegate coordinator, Mr. Glen Rushing, before I left for the Sheraton. Mr. Rushing worked for Mr. Carrol Willis, one of Bill Clinton's Arkansas cohorts, and he was a real insider. (I believe he was one of the Campaign Deputy Directors.) Mr. Rushing had me contact the people in charge of the convention. I met with a very nice person from the Greer Media Consulting Group, and I got my instructions for preparing for the opening night presentation, which was that very night. I had to be at Madison Square Garden by noon that day. It was around 11 a.m. when I cleared the AFL-CIO meeting, and I had the option of taking a taxi to Madison or, as I decided to go, hoofing it.

Since it cost nothing to walk, I got directions and struck out down the street. It was a long walk. No one told me how long a walk it was, or I would have taken a bus or a cab or anything, but I would not have walked. On the other hand, I was in no hurry and it was a beautiful day, so I ambled along taking in the scenery.

As I walked along, despite the fact it was my first time to lay eyes on the place, it had a certain familiarity to it. I couldn't put my finger on it, but I had seen this part of NYC before somewhere. There were theaters everywhere, and the movie houses had these enormous mock-ups, statues as it were, of the characters playing in the movies. The biggest one was at the *Batman Returns* movie house. I looked at the 50-foot high Batman and Penguin and said to myself how this reminded me of the big mock-ups they put on Broadway for grand openings. Then it hit me where I was. I looked around and said, "They say the neon lights are bright on Broadway." Yes, I was smack in the middle of Broadway. No wonder it looked familiar.

It was a truly memorable walk down Broadway that morning. There were all kinds of people out, and no matter what you may have seen, nothing was as diverse as the crowd I crossed paths with that day of July 13th, 1992. On every corner, there was a representative of Jews for Jesus giving out booklets telling about how Jesus died for your sins. I ignored every one of them until this guy absolutely forced me to stop and take a brochure from him. I told him I didn't need any information about Jesus, because I was a Southern Baptist and we wrote the book on Jesus.

I splurged and bought a canned Coke at a convenience store I passed by and felt like a real New Yorker when the guy charged me

$1.25 for it—culture shock in its deadliest form, financial.

As I continued my walk, I came to the place where they lower the big ball on New Year's Eve. I wondered to myself where I would spend this coming New Year's Eve, and then I remembered I would be in Sugar Town down on Bourbon Street, helping paint that "Crescent City So Easy" crimson and white. I was, too, but that's another story.

I could look down the street and see that I was getting close to something, because there were police barricades up—and officers to man them—just down the block. Then I saw it, Madison Square Garden, in all its splendor. It was a good thing too, for I was becoming a bit winded, and by my calculations I still had all of thirteen hours to go before I would be able to get back to the hotel. Since I was there so early, I was able to get in the front door with no delay. I had been wearing my buttons and credentials since I left my room to go to the Sheraton, and I felt so comfortable that I decided that everywhere I went in NYC I would "fly the colors," so to speak.

There were 22 delegates selected to be part of the opening night ceremonies—myself included. Who these 21 other people were, I had no idea, but I was supposed to meet up with them on the convention floor under the sign for "Overseas Delegates." I first had to find the way to the floor of the convention hall. It seemed like I took ramp after ramp—because I did take ramp after ramp—before walking through a portal and into the vastness that is Madison Square proper.

I was prone to a much earthier form of speech then, and as I looked around, a rough-and-tumble form of "wow" came out of my mouth. The place was just like you see on television, all red, white and blue, with the "cracker box" vertical signs displaying the names of the states on them. And there was Alabama! The delegation was right down in front of the stage. Indeed, we were right on the front row. Bob Eucker would have been proud.

I saw a few people standing over by the far wall, and I could tell that perhaps these were some of the other "highlighted" delegates (as we came to be called). One was a beautiful woman of Asian ancestry, and another looked to be a full-blooded Native American. Since there was a very attractive woman involved, I sauntered over and introduced myself. The man was Frank Lemere from Nebraska, and the lovely lady was Jenny Lam from NYC. Both were leaders in their respective communities, and they were really nice people. There was a crew from Nebraska filming Frank, so I waded in and talked politics with them while the camera was cranking. I can imagine we made quite a diverse group: an Asian-American, a Native American, and the Voice of the American worker, J.R. 'Working Man' Hammond.

Everyone had arrived by noon, and it was some crew, let me tell you. We were put through our paces, and the gist of the matter seemed to be that we were to walk up from the convention floor when our name was called out, stand there and look heroic while this truly gifted horn player played "America," and then a chorus was to join in, and we were to exit stage left.

We ran through it twice, and then we were free for the afternoon. The DNC gaveled in at 5 p.m., and we were to go on around 8 p.m. or thereabouts. It was 2 p.m., so I had hours to kill and dang few dollars to help kill it with. There was one highlighted delegate I really became friends with. He was another real leader of America, a man from California, Mr. Ron Gillis.

Ron, when you read this, give yourself a pat on the back because you are the kind of person that makes this country great. I hope we meet again someday. I'm sure we will.

Back to the Garden that July evening.

As had become my custom up there when I had more time than money, I walked around and checked things out. There was a lot going on in this place on that summer day. Anticipation ran high and you could feel the tingle in the air. I was standing in front of the stage, imagining how it was going to feel in a few hours, when I turned around and there was Peter Jennings, star of ABC News. He looks really good in person (in a manly sort of way) and since I had long ago lost my shyness, I walked over and introduced myself. Turns out when he was just starting out in the news business, he covered the part of Alabama in which I live, so we had a common thread that bound us—no matter how slightly.

As I wandered around, afternoon turned into evening. I had many vantage points to look out over the hall, and each was a spectacular view. I eventually got tired of roaming around and was getting thirsty to boot, so I asked a security guard where the employees' lounge was since none of the concession stands was open yet. Once I found out where the working people ate their lunch, I spent some time there every day. By the way, I don't believe I've ever gotten a colder canned drink out of a machine anywhere.

I drank a cold Coke with the people there and got to know some of them. I saw it was 4 p.m., only one hour away from gavel time, so I took off for our spot on the floor and got the aisle seat on the front row at the Democratic National Convention. Needless to say, I felt exhilarated yet drained. By the time they gaveled down the DNC, I had been going and on my feet for eleven hours already, and there was a lot of night to go yet.

Most of the other Alabama delegation had assembled, and I noticed there was some discussion going on behind my back among the "leaders" of the Alabama crowd. They were behind me because I was sitting on the front row and had the best seat in the delegation. Senator Heflin arrived, and he stood around for a few minutes before I was approached by a woman big in Alabama political circles. She told me I should give my front row seat to the Senator. When I looked at her in disbelief—after all, I had gotten there at noon and waited five hours so that I would have that particular seat—she said something about "not wanting to give my seat to the Senior Senator from Alabama," so I got up and gave it to him. I didn't like it, but I did it. Now that I know him, I'd do it not because he's the Senior Senator, but because I know and like him personally.

This was my first real hint that maybe I wasn't as equal as I had been told I was. I figured out later it's a party thing. I hope I get to go to another DNC, because now I know how to handle myself there.

Aretha Franklin began to sing, I looked up at Old Glory, and never in my life have I felt the chills run up and down my spine like they did at that moment. I could feel 200 years of American history and patriotism flowing in my veins, and I began to swell up inside with American pride. Then, I began to cry.

It was more beautiful than anything I had ever experienced and so moving that it brought tears of patriotism, pride, and humility at my being part of such a wonderfully American celebration. As I looked up at our flag, tears streaming down my face, I began to hear cameras going off and the flash attachments were all aimed at my face. I was not about to let anything stop me from looking at the most beautiful flag in history while the queen of soul belted out F. Scott Key's stirring tribute to American courage, valor, and virtues. It seemed like there were a thousand pictures being taken of me, and I have no way of knowing in how many newspapers the different photos of me crying during the National Anthem appeared. I know it was in the Tuesday, July 14, 1992, edition of *The New York Daily News*, and I have a copy of it somewhere. Come by sometime and I'll show you.

As I said, I love this country. I was up there to try and make a better nation for myself and all the other working people who had other things to do (like raising a family, paying bills and taxes, and being good, productive, American citizens).

I figure different groups in America have their champions, and I, by golly, was going to champion the cause of the grass roots, blue collar, American Worker. I am still doing it by writing this book. There is no one to speak for us that is really one of us. Once you become a big leader, you are not really one of us any more. That is what is so important about me standing in the front row of the DNC. I was the only one of us up there, folks, and I felt it was quite a responsibility.

I listened to the proceedings for an hour, and then thirst and hunger drove me to action. I had to have something to eat and drink or I would surely be unable to handle the proceedings coming up in 90 minutes, at 8:30 p.m. I headed for the concession stands that I had noticed in my wanderings during the day. They weren't manned earlier, but now there was a beehive of activity as everyone there seemed to want a Coke and a hot dog at the same time. I then hurt my chin again because when I looked up and saw the total cost for a hot dog and a Coke, my mouth snapped open in an involuntary gasp. If I got a bag of chips also, the total would come to nearly $10! I turned away and did a slow and sad walk.

I don't know if I mentioned it or not, but if I did, I'll tell you again; I read all the literature they gave out to each delegate, and I have this knack for remembering trivia, odds and ends, and phone numbers. As I walked along the corridor, passing all the happy people who were not hungry and thirsty, I was thinking, if this doesn't beat all. I had no idea it was going to be this tough being the Voice of the American Worker. I can take the physical strain, but this not being able to afford a hot dog really sucks. I don't even like hot dogs, and here I can't afford to buy one—not if I plan to stretch my money until Friday, anyhow. And after all that great stuff I had last night, it's too bad there's not a party going on now down here.

Then I remembered something. Didn't I read about a hospitality suite for elected Democratic officials? Yeah, all the big cats who can afford a thousand hot dogs are getting to eat for free just because they are elected Democratic officials. I bet the food down there is the best in the building, maybe the city! And it's free! It's just not fair. It's too bad I don't live in a city, for maybe then I could be a Democratic mayor or a city councilman or something. But no, I had to live in the country where there are nothing but trees. Yes, it's too bad there's no actual city of Woodstock, Alabama.

Although—I was thinking to myself—nobody in New York but me actually knows that there is no city of Woodstock, Alabama. And I really am not in the mood for a hot dog, anyway. How about it, Mr. Mayor? Mr. J. R. 'Working Man' Hammond just got elected mayor of the previously nonexistent city of Woodstock, Alabama, and he is our first elected representative. Yeah, I think if I act sincere, I can pull this off. All right Mr. Mayor, let's go get some dinner.

I headed over to a security guard to find out where this hospitality suite was located. With directions in hand and a peachy idea in my mind, away I went on my quest for justice, truth, the American way of life, and a free dinner.

Turning a corner, I found myself facing a table of several young folks backed up by the ever-present security guards. When I saw their eager faces looking up at me, ready to assist the elected democratic leaders of America, I knew that if I just played it cool, I was in.

I walked up with a bold and assured stride and inquired in a clear and authoritarian voice, "Is this the hospitality suite for elected democratic officials?"

A man and woman, each around 20, seemed to be in charge of the operation.

"Why yes it is," they both replied and nodded back at me.

"Well, how are you this grand and glorious evening? I'm J. R. Hammond, and I've come to check out this little ol' hospitality room you've set up for us elected types."

They looked puzzled and asked my name and started consulting some lists they had. Strangely, my name was not on them! They had no record of me at all, and asked just what my office was.

"Why, I'm the Mayor of Woodstock, Alabama. I'm the first Democratic mayor we've ever had." (Which was true, considering the fact that we don't have a town, and the only government building we have is our U.S. Post Office.)

"I haven't been in office long." (Which was also true, since I only thought up the office five minutes earlier.)

"It was a real close election, and in fact I only won by one vote." (Despite the narrow margin, I would like to point out that I did receive 100 percent of the votes cast.)

"It's a real pleasure to be here." (Which was especially true.)

They talked among themselves for a minute and then asked if I had anything with my name on it saying I was mayor of Woodstock. I told them "no, I haven't been mayor long enough to have any official cards printed up, and besides, we are a very poor town, and I have to work a second job because my salary as mayor isn't enough to live on." (That was also all true enough.)

I finally pulled out my driver's license and showed them I did, indeed, live in Woodstock, Alabama. I told them, "Look, I'm tired, hungry, and thirsty. I've been here since 12 noon practicing for my part in the opening night ceremonies, and I am due on stage in one hour. By the way, the people in Little Rock really love me. If you want, let's go to a phone and you can call my secretary Elesha back there in Woodstock who will verify my recent election. Or, I can call the Clinton people and tell them that you two are not letting me have dinner, and they will send someone here to instruct you both in political protocol. Whatever you decide, do it quick, because like I just told you, my part in tonight's opening ceremony starts in one hour."

They immediately said, "No, no, Mr. Mayor, you can go in, but you must sign in on this special list and after tonight there will be no more signing up like this." "Does this mean I'll have to go through all this crap every night?" I shot back at them, my voice bristling with righteous indignation. "Oh, no, Mr. Mayor, sir, you are good for the entire DNC. Go down the steps, and when you get to the bottom you'll see a door to your right. Enjoy!"

I turned my back to them, and the straight face I had fought so hard to maintain dissolved into a big Woodstock, Alabama, grin.

# CHAPTER 17

## Dinner with the V.I.P.s, a little football talk, and my time in the spotlight

As I opened the door and looked in, my eyes took in the type of scene seldom if ever witnessed by ordinary working folk. Except, of course, for those working there as food and drink servers. I had just entered a world off limits to 99.99 percent of the American population. A world where all the leadership of the National Democratic Party—the Congressmen, Senators, and Governors—went to celebrate their return to battle as they met to fire the first shot in the 51st political war for the White House. The first two such events were uncontested. The rest have been anything but. So this was one more meeting of the minds, one more tribal council preceding the campaign to occupy 1600 Pennsylvania Avenue. If there was any place with more power per table than the V.I.P. hospitality suite for elected Democratic officials, it must have been some palaver.

As I walked over to the bar in the middle of the first room to get a Coke, I looked around and everywhere I looked I saw people of authority eating, drinking, and having a big time together in a most relaxed atmosphere. I honestly think most of the American Democratic leaders where in that room that night, except for the Governor of Arkansas and his pal, Al.

I bristled with pride at the thought that in this country, the mayor of a small, nonexistent, Southern town with a population of two was welcome to party with the big cats in their leisure time. And there were no bodyguards or security people in with us, as we were the cream of Democratic society and could let our hair down around each other in the perfect security that the person next to you has just as much to lose as you do if word gets out what you've been doing.

I finally got a much-needed Coke from the ultra-busy bartender, and I started off towards the far end of the bar room and kept going until I walked right into the banquet room. When a regular guy is in the company of the elite, and gets to live like they live and eat like they eat, even spectacular food sometimes is underrated and its uniqueness is overlooked. But if I ever again eat food that tasted as good as that did that night, I'll be surprised. I guess it tasted so good because I was being caught up in the spirit of the moment. Aides to our next President were telling me I was a part of things in a big way and would be so after the election. I was soon going to be on stage at the DNC on nationwide TV. I had been going all day without a meal or a break, but mainly I think it was a combination of the food being awfully good, and the fact I had just elected myself mayor of Woodstock, Alabama, that made the meal so unforgettable. Whatever the reason, or combinations thereof, I got in line and prepared myself to be dazzled, both by the food and the company.

The opulence of the buffet was first-rate, the best. The atmosphere, the ambience, and everything else, put me in a most convivial mood. As the line moved along, I counted ten chef-type people dishing out the offerings. And then I saw the actual spread, and it was incredible.

Every kind of bakery product, dessert, fruit, and cheese was laid out for our enjoyment. And this guy was carving up a slab of prime rib as long as your arm. He cut me a very respectable slice and handed the plate towards me. As nice as it was, it wasn't nearly close to the size I needed.

"That little piece of beef looks very lonely to me. Why don't you put another piece next to it to keep it company?" He looked very puzzled for a brief moment, smiled, and added another slice to my plate after telling me "bon appetite." Then as I moved further up the line, I added some veggies and inspected the items at the end of the table. There was a group of New York ethnic delicacies, so I had some of each. The Italian sausage and green peppers were simply unforgettable.

I headed for a table to eat this fabulous repast, and I found one in the bar room. I ate with the gusto and pleasure of those eating the best food in town in a truly special place. It went down awesomely well. I finished everything on my plate, and relaxed for a moment as I thought of how I was going to be on stage in just a few minutes. I was mentally and physically ready, and confidence filled me. I decided to get one more Coke before I headed back to the convention floor.

I walked up next to a man wearing a very nice suit. He looked at me and nodded hello, and I said "hi!" back and politely waited for the barkeep to come around.

As I casually looked at the man, I noticed he had a "I heart South Carolina" button on his chest. I said to him, "So you're from South Carolina, huh? Well, you guys have finally moved up to the big leagues football-wise. It will be hard to compete this first year, I know. Alabama has a monster team this year, and they'll win it all and be national champs."

At this, he and I talked football for ten minutes or so. He told me his name but it didn't ring a bell with me. I guess mine didn't ring a bell with him, either. I had finished my Coke and was getting ready to head out for real when I turned to tell this S.C. football fan "so long and good luck."

As I shook his hand good-bye, a thought crossed my mind. Everybody here but me was somebody big in the Party. Who was this guy? I said "So you're from South Carolina, huh? Are you the Governor of South Carolina?" He shook his head and said, "No, we have a Republican Governor." He hesitated a moment and then added, smiling, "I'm the Lieutenant Governor, though."

With that, I burst out laughing (no doubt causing the Lieutenant Governor of South Carolina to wonder just who let me in there). I told him it was nice to meet him, and that I was "Working Man" Hammond, the newly elected mayor of Woodstock, Alabama. Shaking hands again, now a personal acquaintance of the highest ranking Democrat in South Carolina, I headed out of this den of supreme Americana.

Before I leave the hospitality suite, let me ask you this question. How often do you think any politician of note, somebody with a big territory—like the Lieutenant Governor of South Carolina—speaks to someone at a bar about football for ten minutes without having the other person know who he is? How often do the leaders of this country hear what the average person thinks about things? I'll tell you, seldom to never.

I am jumping ahead now to 1994, but this is one of the problems the Clinton administration is having. They have little input from anyone who is not a lawyer and/or from the Ivy League. But we'll get into this later in the book. I have a lot to say about our new President that I worked so hard to help elect.

Anyway, back to the Lieutenant Governor of that proud and truly Southern state, South Carolina.

I sensed an air of amusement when he had to tell me who he was. I can understand how our leaders are prisoners of their own success, and they are just not able to get out and meet people incognito (as they must be protected from the lunatic fringe). He and I were two guys that met in a bar and had a man-to-man chat about something that is discussed nationwide by millions of pairs of guys who just happen to meet at a bar. He seems like a real nice guy. I hope to meet him again sometime though who knows if our paths will cross. He sure had on a nice suit.

As I made my way back to the convention floor, the situation was becoming intense. Things were happening on stage, and the young black singer, Reggie Jackson, was about to go on. He was to sing "America the Beautiful," and then it was to be our time. As Reggie put his great voice to use, we "highlighted" delegates lined up on either side of the stage, ready to ascend and have our fifteen minutes of fame.

When the other members of the Alabama delegation realized I was going up on the stage, they were stunned, excited, and totally happy for me. People were asking, "Why didn't you say you were going on stage?" I said "Surprise! I'm going on stage!"

I had become part of the group, what with my going to the museum party, not making any trouble, and holding my own in such elevated company. At least I felt like I did, and as the delegates started moving up from the floor, I got ready for my cue to go on.

As the first five delegates in this little part of the democratic process were called forth and walked up from the floor, there was a very dignified silence. When they called my name and I walked up from the floor, there was a burst of spontaneous applause. I got to my spot there in the very center of the stage, and they were still cheering me so I turned towards them, raised my right arm up in the air, and gave a victory salute to the members of the Alabama delegation.

By the way, I have a nice video copy of the proceedings, courtesy of the Frank Greer Consulting Firm, the group who handled the Clinton campaign media effort. As fate would have it, everybody's picture except mine was shown up on the big wall of televisions at the back of the stage. Big, giant, monster-sized photos of the delegates were shown nationwide as they walked up from the floor, all except mine because the camera crew was still on the previous person. But I was in a lot of other shots during the time we were on

*I had a great time roaming around
the convention floor, meeting and
talking to people and making new friends in other delegations.*

stage, so any working people who were taking this in did get to see
their representative up there with the soon-to-be President Clinton
for forty minutes or so.

As I reached the part of the DNC "Salute To Delegates" where
I had to stand and smile a lot, I looked out over the audience and
decided this was a very sharp place to be. And, if you were watching
the right channel, you got to see a totally nonpolitical person being
called to the center of the stage at a Democratic National Convention. You got to see a laid-off coal miner being saluted by Democrats all over America. I walked up from the convention floor on the

right side of the stage wearing my blue dress shirt and blue jeans, dressed as a true representative of working-class America, and I assumed a position directly in the middle of the stage.

It was a moment I look back on with pride, not just because it was me, but because some average person had gotten involved in this campaign at a level high enough to have some input and access to the future Clinton administration. (Or so I was being told at the time by those in the Clinton camp.)

I had run as the Working Man, and had become an important delegate to the DNC. I was the only average American I could see there at the DNC, and I was not beholden to any group in American society except that group of which I am a lifelong member, blue-collar, working-for-a-living, middle class America. I stand for those people who have to work for a living and take care of their families. I represent those who pay their taxes, and who—while being toler-ant—have been pushed to the wall by faulty government and wealth-oriented leaders that allowed billions of dollars to be stolen by people like them from people just like you and me. In fact, it was you and I who footed the bill for the "Crime of the Century," the ransacking of the savings and loans institutions.

There were 16 more delegates who came up after me. Each man and woman that stood alongside me that night was a gracious and intelligent individual, and it was a pleasure to meet and share the stage with them all. I did my best to enjoy it.

After we were all assembled, our part was over except for the standing and waiting for someone to tell us it was time to leave. The man who played the trumpet came on with "America," and a choir came on and sang. Then it was time to go, and so we left the stage. It was really cool, though, being in the spotlight for a moment. I'm sure you can appreciate something like this if you work for a living. It's not often we are included in such things. We are just too busy making a living to be involved.

We left the stage and entered a long corridor that ran the length of the floor and emptied out into the hall I always used to go and come from our part of the floor. When I got back to the Alabama delegation, I was well received. Evidently, they got a real kick out of one of their own getting special attention.

I spent the rest of the evening watching the events on stage, listening to speeches, and smiling a lot. There were big celebrities making appearances all night in the California delegation, which was located adjacent to and directly behind the Alabama gang. The most beautiful and charming Mary Steenburgen was a California delegate and made an appearance every night. In fact, Richard Dreyfuss, Buck Henry, and a host of the Hollywood crowd were frequent visitors to the California area. But Mary Steenburgen and I became actual acquaintances later on in the convention.

The rest of the opening night, Monday, July 13th, 1992, was a bit anticlimactic for me, since I was still excited after having been on the stage. However, there was a lot of talent. The best, I thought, was Mac Davis doing Will Rogers. It was a really great piece of show-manship.

When all the events for Monday night at the DNC had ground to a halt, the Alabama delegation left as a whole and headed back to the Loews, where a final opening night treat was to be the pent-house party thrown for the Alabama delegation and friends by the Governor of Alabama, James Folsom.

I was in a buoyant mood, to say the least. I had met every challenge thrown at me and had been the star of the Alabama delegation on opening night. I was a most warmly received indi-vidual that night by those from Alabama and the Kansas and North Carolina folks who were bunked with us there at the Loews. It was a night I'll not soon forget.

After I had freshened up, I headed for the penthouse. Governor Folsom had a very inviting spread laid out for us. It was after midnight, and everyone was coming up and congratulating me for being on stage that night. I must say, the rest of the delegation became friendlier all at once. I really enjoyed getting to know every person I met in New York and on the campaign trail.

He had a really swinging band hired, so live music was the evening staple. I passed through the buffet because I had had a really long day, and I'll be darned if I'm going to get around free food and not eat. I grabbed a drink and headed for the dance area, which was the same room in which we got our credentials every morning (minus the chairs). The band was playing some good sounds that early July morning, and I sipped my vodka on the rocks and watched the rest of the Alabama delegation party down.

We danced and made merry for a while, and then when most of the people that mattered had arrived, the big cats got together at the microphone and sang what they called the "Official Alabama DNC Theme Song." Now, it was late, I was tired, and my hearing is not what it used to be. I may have some words mixed up, but this is the gist of the song. It's sung to the tune of "Take Me Out To The Ball Game."

THE OFFICIAL DEMOCRATIC NATIONAL
CONVENTION ALABAMA DELEGATION THEME SONG

Let's have parties and banquets,
Parties, banquets and balls.

Jack Kennedy kept
us all out of war.
Let's get together
And party some more.

And we'll all have parties and banquets,
Parties, banquets and balls,

We'll have parties and banquets
And banquets and parties
And balls, balls, balls!

I smiled and sang along with the crowd, and the stray thought crossed my mind; what would the working people of Alabama think if they knew that all the people they had elected to come up here and make it a better nation were singing songs about party-hearty time in New York?

Anyway, it was really neat being around the Alabama Big Dogs when they let their hair down. The party finally drew to a close, and, as I was leaving, a papier-maché Democratic donkey decoration did a swan dive into my arms, so I was forced to take it to my room and give it a place to stay.

I drifted down to the lounge to close out the evening, sitting around with the guys and feeling more a part of things than I had a right to. I became friends with Billy Joe Camp, a mainstay in Alabama politics for many years. He is a truly fine individual, and his stories of his years as George Wallace's press secretary were fascinating. It is my pleasure to know Billy Joe Camp.

My long day had finally taken its toll on my body, and as there were nothing but men in the bar, I had made ready to actually turn in when this pretty woman came in to the hotel lobby and drifted over by the bar. It was about 3 a.m., so I was surprised at her late hours. She walked by me, so I smiled and said hello. She responded with a big smile and said, "Hello, Baby." I asked her if she'd like to party, my fatigue leaving instantly at the prospect of spending some time with this pretty lady. She got right in my face and said, "Yes, let's go up to your room." That's when I realized she was being a little too friendly too quickly.

I asked her if she was a pro, and she told me, "Yes, a girl's got to make a living." I agreed with the making a living part but assured her I was the most economically disadvantaged delegate in New York. She smiled, told me I didn't know what I was missing, and headed out for greener pastures. The last time I saw her she was talking to this guy about 60 years old, and he sure seemed to be having a good time. New York is something else. It's the only foreign country I've ever been to.

# CHAPTER 18

## Women and me(n) and Tuesday night poetry

Tuesday, July 14th, was Women's Night at the DNC. It was also the night the of the Major League All Star Baseball Game, or so I was told; I missed it being at the DNC that night.

That morning when I awakened after my three hours sleep, I got ready for the day and headed for the penthouse to meet with the delegation and get my Tuesday night credentials. It was this routine every day, meeting over a cup of coffee and discussing the events of the preceding evening. And this morning in the Alabama delegation, I was one of the hot topics due to my being part of the opening night ceremonies.

All of a sudden, I wasn't an outsider anymore. It was a definite change for the better. It was very nice to have people in positions of power, people whom I had read about and seen on the news for years, come to know me by name and for me to know them. I got neck-hugs from a U.S. Senator and the Governor of Alabama later wrote me a letter telling me I was now a personal friend of his.

Heavy stuff for a coal miner, yet at the time I had become one with these people, and I had tried to carry myself in a manner befitting my role as representative of the American worker, especially concerning our being a part of the Clinton team. I was a part of it, and I had earned my place on the team without help from anyone else. My success was largely from luck, mostly due to Ross Perot, and because of this I actually was indebted to no one in the Alabama Democratic Party. Of course, some people didn't like the fact that I had not paid my dues—both financially and in years of service—to the Democratic Party, and yet I was the one being patted on the back by the Alabama delegation to the DNC.

In fact, while it's all hearsay, another Alabama delegate told me this little item. A lot of time and effort was spent getting the Alabama Democratic mascot, Irene the Donkey, up to New York for the DNC. This kind of stuff plays well in the press. But after I made my splash, one of the leaders of the Alabama Democratic Party said to some of the regular Party members, "I can't believe it. All this trouble to get this donkey up here and a G**-damn coal miner steals the show."

But you can see how those that really are part of the Democratic Party could be jealous of an outsider like myself. By the way, don't worry about Irene; she got even later.

There was a light breakfast for us every morning: sweet rolls, crescent rolls, eggs (some mornings), but no more chefs serving omelettes. What a pity. However, since there was something, and it was free, I managed to start off every day on a full stomach.

I spent Tuesday walking the streets of New York, checking out the town as best I could without spending any money. I heard everyone else's plans at the penthouse meeting, and they had baseball games to go to and shopping to do, sight-seeing, and Broadway plays to make. Sounded good to me, too, and if I ever go back, I'll try to do the same myself.

By that evening, I was in great spirits and raring to go. I had an actual schedule conflict that evening, as did every Alabama delegate. We had been invited to the truly great house of an Alabama native who lived in New York for a B-B-Q and moon pie dinner, but the hours conflicted with the Convention. I would have liked to attend both, but I was not in New York to tour the mansions of million-aires, but to try and represent the American workers as best I could, so I missed the mansion and B-B-Q.

I invited a fellow delegate from another state to come to dinner with me at the hospitality suite for elected Democratic officials, and so she joined me. I had met her there in Madison Square Garden and ran around with her some. She told me she worked for a financial institution. I got her past the kids at the check-in desk by saying she was the wife of the Democratic mayor of Woodstock, Alabama. It was another good meal, although not as extravagant as the first night.

While talking over dinner, I casually asked her where she went to school. This simple question actually broke up our relationship. She hesitated a bit before answering. She looked at me and said, "You really want to know?" I said sure, though at that moment I wasn't so sure. "Well, I got my bachelor's degree at Harvard and my master's at Yale." I felt ignorant by comparison. I asked what her job was, and she said she was a vice president of the company. So I—a laid-off, broke coal miner who didn't know how he was going to pay his mortgage that month—was dining unknowingly with a woman who was, by my standards, rich. There was no reason for her to be impressed with having dinner in the hospitality suite. She ate with people like that every day and could probably buy and sell me at will. She was a very nice lady, but after she explained more about herself to me, I realized I could not impress her in a dozen conventions and decided not to press the issue with her any further.

And what issue is that, you might ask, and I'd tell you this: man-woman issues. You see, I am single, and I think women are great. I am a fool for a pretty face.

I counted 27 different women with whom I interacted at the Convention. Now I was raised by my mom and my grandmother, God rest her soul. I am raising my daughter, Elesha, and I consider women the embodiment of everything good about the human race.

I have been around enough to know that there are things that transcend the boundaries of politics, economics, science, religion and the metaphysical. My favorite one of them is male-female interaction.

The boy-meets-girl scenario has been around since prehistory, and as long as men and women get together in any way, shape, form, or fashion, it will continue. I am a champion of women's rights, but as I tell my most amazing and incredible daughter, even Madame Curie had a fella.

So, despite the fact that I was in New York solely to advance the status of working-class America, I am 100 percent American male, and I am a single man who sees nothing wrong with finding out, in a civilized and friendly manner, if a woman wants to get to know you better. And so I did. It never hurts to advertise.

That Tuesday night at the DNC, I spent a lot of time roaming around, seeing what I could get into. I listened to all the fine women speakers that night, as I visited different delegations and checked out the action. As I said earlier, I met Peter Jennings of ABC News the opening night of the DNC, and he is a real prince of a guy. As I mentioned, he told me when he first started out in the news business that his beat was Mississippi and central Alabama, and he had been through the Tuscaloosa area many times. It was great meeting you, Peter Jennings. I'm the guy who on two different nights tried to have my picture taken with you, only to have my flash not work.

I noticed some commotion around 9 p.m., and I decided to drift back over by the Alabama group. This was the night the Jerry Brown forces were marching up and down the aisles saying "Let Jerry Speak." By the next night, some guy had made up a sign with a picture of Jerry Lewis on it wearing one of his really stupid hats and expressions. Next to the photo, he had written, "Let Jerry Speak." Below it he had the caption, "50 Million Frenchmen Can't Be Wrong." It made the national news. It was great. I went over and told him I thought it was really cool.

That night being women's night, a lot of the truly fine Alabama women—including two of the most charming and delightful women it has been my pleasure to encounter, Mrs. Howell Heflin and Mrs. Tom Bevill—were sitting on the front row of our section of the Garden. The aisles were becoming packed with people, and they were actually crushing down on Mrs. Heflin and Mrs. Bevill, and as I walked up, I was asked by some of the delegation to stand around them and act as a human wall to keep these Brown folk away from our women.

This was a good job for me as I was not fond of these Brown radicals, anyway. In fact, one of them tried to get tough with me and even cursed me like the S.M.Y.B. did at the Planet Hollywood club. Lucky for him my good nature took hold, and I just laughed at him.

I had taken a few minutes to shove out those that had infringed on our sovereign territory, and I had given our women a little breathing room. I, in effect, became a buttress, unyielding and unforgiving. I let no one close to those flowers of the South. It was hot and hectic, but the smile Mrs. Heflin gave me when she had breathing room made it all worthwhile.

By 10:30, things had become more normal, and I drifted back away from the stage. I was watching a speech when I saw a guy come by with a video camera, filming as he went. I flagged him down and asked him who he was with. He was a cameraman for the PBS show called "The Nineties," and he told me they were doing a special on the DNC. I said, "Hey! Interview me!" And so he did. It was shown during prime time on the night of September 25th, and it wasn't half bad. It was my only nationwide interview, and it may have gotten Clinton elected. You can look at me, listen to what I had to say, and realize that my words rang with a truth born of hard work in the depths of the Earth and years of raising my daughter alone.

I had moved into a standing position on a chair so I could better see things when I had an encounter with a beautiful young woman. She was standing in the chair next to me and was in the act of falling on her head when I reached out and snatched her out of the air. With my arm firmly around her waist, I deposited her back onto her chair. I steadied her with my other hand, and as she regained her balance and composure, I ended up being face to face with her and my arms around her. "Well hello, there, little darling. Are you all right? Are you okay?" She told me she was and thanked me.

This was the first young, beautiful woman I had had in my arms in a while, so I was in no hurry to get away from her. "Why don't you and I go party?" She told me she couldn't, so I turned her loose. I asked her where she went to school, and it was one of the Ivy League schools. (Boy, did I get tired of meeting people from there.) And she was on the floor because her dad got her a pass. I asked, "Is your father rich?" "Oh, yes, and immensely so," was her answer.

By 11 p.m., things were nearly done for the evening, and I was standing back out of the way. There was a guy next to me wearing one of those Jewish hats on the back of his head. Being the friendly guy that I am, I struck up a conversation, and we spoke for several minutes about several things including Israel, the election, and who I was. I told him I was glad that Israel was on our side, and that we in the mines appreciated any country that could kick butt the way Israel could.

We agreed that something had to be done to normalize things somehow with the Arabs. I finally introduced myself to him, and he told me his name was Rhom Shapiro. He was the head fund raiser for the Democratic Party, and he had raised a million dollars for them the previous night. At the time, I really didn't realize just how powerful he was.

He and I talked further until things were about to gavel down for the evening. He then turned to me and said he had invitations to two parties after the DNC shut down for the evening, and that he could only go to one of them, and would I be interested in going to a party at the top of the Chrysler Building?

I told him I could probably work it into my schedule, and he gave me a red, printed invitation that he had. We shook hands and told each other how nice it was to meet each other and then parted company. The next day when I was talking to the Clinton staffer that I had been dealing with—the one who told me "They love you in Little Rock!"—I told him about meeting this guy named Rhom Shapiro. He said that he was one of the top Democratic Party leaders in the country and their chief fund raiser. I have since seen him on C-Span and other news programs. I enjoyed meeting you, pal, and I really hate not getting to know you better.

I made it back to the hotel without further incident. I showered and dressed and was on my way to the Chrysler Building. But as was the custom by now, almost everyone in the Alabama delegation was meeting in the lounge to discuss the events of the evening. They also had one of those Karaoke things where the people in the audience sang along to recorded music, and they were taping each partici- pant.

I headed towards the lobby, and blew into the bar that takes up most of the ground floor there in the Loews Hotel. Some of the guys had already gathered there, as it had become the custom to meet informally and discuss events of the evening and generally unwind. I told them to guess where I was fixing to head out to. None could, and when I showed them the invite to the Chrysler Building, they were duly (or maybe dully) impressed. I put it on the bar next to me, and turned away from the bar to talk to a reporter. When I turned back, to my horror, my invitation was gone!

I wonder if I would have had to write this book if I had attended that party. I guess we'll never know. The bartender had wiped the bar, and into the garbage went my hopes for that night. Since I couldn't go to the Chrysler party, I did the next best thing and joined the one going on there at the hotel.

Besides the general enjoyment of being the star of the show, they had sweetened the pot by offering a free trip to Los Angeles. for the best singer. I can't sing very well, and unless I write the song so it is within my limited range, I don't even attempt it. There was a woman from Alabama who kept trying to get me to sing. She was insistent and endearing. Your husband is a lucky man, indeed, to have you for a mate.

But as I watched the show, I knew that this crowd was going to hear something no other bunch—outside the state of Alabama— had been exposed to, my poetry.

I write poetry, you see. Working-class poetry. Not highbrow poetry, but poetry that the working people of this land can get into.

I had become a trouper, as far as being in front of the crowd, and was not the least bit camera shy. So I walked over to the M.C. and asked him if I could do one of my poems. He pointed at the mike, and told me to go for it.

So I did my most famous poem. You get to hear it, too.

### ODE TO A SECOND DIVORCE

As I speak to you, I'm filled with remorse.
  I've just finished getting my second divorce.

When I told the judge I wanted half,
  He looked at me and started to laugh.

He gave her our car;
  He gave her our home.

He gave me my toothbrush
  And gave me my comb.

I said "That's okay, Judge, I've still got my shoes."
  He said "My mistake," and he gave her them, too.

And as she drove away, no longer my wife,
  She said, "One more sucker like you, and I'm set for life!"

The large happy crowd seemed so appreciative of good poetry, that I was forced to do another of my works, this one in commemoration of a man who didn't realize his limitations and suffered because of it.

### LITTLE BIGHORN REVISITED

This poem's for you,
General George Armstrong Custer,
Though a century has passed,
You've not lost your luster.

And we still in reverence,
Of that ill-fated morn,
When they cut off your hair
At the Little Big Horn.

Would hair dye have saved you,
Custer old fellow?

Would Clairol have saved
Your long Hair of yellow?

And the scalp it was attached to,
And the rest of your men.
You carried your butt
Where it shouldn't have been.

Well, Custer, you've been dead an awful long time,
And I'm getting close to the end of my rhyme.
Your demise taught us one thing that we can't ignore,
When it comes to your hair it's best to make love, not war!

I like this poem. I have videotapes of my two efforts at sharing my creations with the world. The second one has me sharing the screen with a prominent Alabama political leader. He is behind me with a big "Not" sign from the convention. He's never seen it. It is amusing.

I got back to the bar, and I was sitting there drinking my water. It had been a long night, and it was around 1:30 a.m., and the festivities and the crowd had dwindled down, so I decided to call it an evening. And then . . .

. . . Every beautiful woman who had been the dream of every man that ever called himself an American came into view, wearing a red dress and lipstick to match. She had dark hair like that most famous Southern belle, Scarlett O'Hara. She was the American beauty rose, that most lovely American flower, in human form. She was a woman with an air of sophistication and class about her unmatched in the annals of male-female encounters—mine, anyway.

She walked into the lobby wearing that red dress and a look of confidence born through years of looking into the mirror and seeing herself. She was the most beautiful woman I had ever seen.

Boy, I thought, I must have had too much water. No one could look that good at this hour of the night. Now I see what Roy Orbison was talking about. To my amazement, she turned and headed towards the lounge, and sat down by herself at the other end of the bar! It suddenly came to me that this work of art was sitting at the bar by herself, and I was at the bar by myself, and maybe I should think about talking to her.

There were a few other men dressed in their suits and sharp clothes. I had my tiger-striped Alabama hat on, as ever, and was wearing somewhat relaxed clothing. I sat there and waited to see who would make a move on her. I waited for them to act. None of them did! I don't get out much. I am home every night that my daughter is, and she is home 90 percent of the time. I don't date much because I won't go out and leave her home by herself. She feels better, and I feel better. Anyway, I'm home a lot. I meet few pretty women in the circles I run in, and no beautiful ones. To be this close to a woman of movie-star looks was very exciting. And nobody in the bar was trying to talk to her.

Now I realized that she was there because she wanted to be with people; and I was a person! Before my meteoric rise in the Democratic Party, before I went from being an ordinary coal miner to being the voice of the American worker, I might have sat there and not done anything. But now, I represented 200 million Americans, and half of these were men. And every one of them would have wanted me to go over and talk to this woman. And so I did.

I walked up to her, and reached out and tapped her on the shoulder. She turned around, and it was like the blast of an exploding supernova. It was as though the Mona Lisa had come to life. She was amazingly beautiful up close.

She looked up at me, kinda cocked her head a little and said, "Yes?"

I said, "Excuse me, ma'am. My name is J. R. 'Working Man' Hammond. I'm from Woodstock, Alabama, and I'm a delegate up here for the Democratic National Convention. I got elected by accident, I'm not in politics, and I'm a full-time parent to my teenage daughter, Elesha. I work in the coal mines, and I'm the only person up here to represent working-class America. And, ma'am, every working man in America would be mad at me if I didn't come over here and tell you that you are, without a doubt, the most beautiful woman in the world. You're a painting, ma'am, a work of art. Boy, that dress is really something. With your dark hair and that red lipstick on, you look like the lady in red that got John Dillinger killed. Are you dangerous to be around? I don't care. I could face death willingly for a woman like you. You must really enjoy looking in a mirror and seeing yourself. Heaven knows, you have a right to. Jesus, did you know your eyes actually shine? Well, it's been nice meeting you. Although since I didn't get your name, I don't guess I actually met you."

She looked me in the eyes while I was talking to her, and her big brown eyes seem to sparkle and dance as she listened to my impassioned plea for her approval. When I finished speaking, she looked at me for another moment, then said, "You're really good, you know that? Sit down."

Bells rang out across the land; rockets were launched and climbed to the heights, before exploding into aerial illustrations of incredible intensity; around the world, the forces of good and justice battled the forces of chaos and evil.

But here in the bar of the Loews Hotel on Lexington Avenue in New York City on a Tuesday night—Wednesday morning—I could care less. I had just been asked to sit down and talk to a woman so good-looking as to intimidate those suit-boys that were still there in the bar with me. She was a woman I would have done anything for after one minute's conversation with her.

I sat down. At that moment, sitting down took on a whole new meaning. Sitting down was a victory the likes of which I had never been exposed to before. I had been around a lot of average-looking women; I had been around a few good-looking women; and I had enjoyed an encounter or two with very attractive women.

But never in my wildest dreams did I ever imagine I would spend time with a woman that looked like this one. I saw some outtakes from *Gone With The Wind* of Vivian Leigh playing to the camera and flirting with the lens. When she would look into the lens and tilt her head and glance demurely with that come-on look in her eye, it would have melted the heart of any man.

And we talked. She was as intelligent a person as I had ever been around, and then some. We talked about our lives. Hers was a lot better sounding than mine. She was wealthy, and had her own company. I told her about my life as a parent/worker/voice of American worker, and she listened to every word of it as though it was fascinating. I kept talking because I was afraid she would leave.

After a while, I realized she was above all else, a lady. And ladies sitting in a bar at 3 a.m talking to a total stranger are fair game in my book. So, I asked her if she would like to come up to my room. She told me she was flattered, but she actually had a husband back home, and she didn't fool around. I told her I could respect that but would she make an exception just this once. She laughed and said no chance, but if it made me feel better, I could continue asking and she wouldn't be offended. So for the next one and a half hours, I put into words everything in my soul, everything in my heart, everything that I could come up with as to why we should share sensuous secrets of the universe. She seemed most amused by the whole thing.

Around 4:30 a.m., she told me she was hungry, and asked if I would like to walk with her up the street to an all-night deli. The idea of accompanying this lovely lady through the bowels of hell itself would have sounded good that night, so I said "lead on, fair princess" and away we went.

When we hit the street, we turned away from the Waldorf Astoria and walked side-by-side under a moon the size of Cleveland. After a minute, I reached over and took her hand in mine, and she let me. Hand in hand, roots-of-grass and upper-class America strolled down Lexington Avenue in as unusual a duo as has ever graced New York.

When we reached the deli, I opened the door for her and followed her to the "Order Here" sign where she ordered a "pastrami on white with mustard," and a Coke. As I watched her eat, I found myself realizing the end had to be near. I hated watching each bite as it disappeared into her flawless mouth, and slide down that throat that I would have fought anything to protect.

She told me she was a vegetarian normally, but she had spent a lot of time in N.Y.C. when she was young and beautiful and in school and just wanted a New York deli sandwich. I could only look at her but could not imagine how perfection could look any more beautiful.

I told her, "You may have looked younger, but the laws of physics, nature, and mathematics preclude you from having looked any more beautiful. You are amazingly alluring. You are Cleopatra. Marilyn Monroe on her best days couldn't hold a candle to you. I only hope that you think of me sometimes, and remember the man you met that didn't care about your money, your education, or anything, the man who fell in love with you on a summer night in New York. Remember me, sweet Scarlett. For as surely as the sun will rise today, this night with you will go down as the high point of my life."

She laughed and told me I should be writing fiction for a living. When she had finished her sandwich, we once again hit the avenue. I didn't grab her hand this time, as she walked next to me on our way back to the hotel. No, I looked over at her and she was looking at me and smiling. She then told me, "I won't forget you, J.R. Trust me on that." As she smiled at me and I reached out for her, I put my arm around her, and held her near as we walked back to the hotel.

When we reached the lobby, she told me she was now officially tired and was going up to her room. I told her I'd go along and see her to her door.

The elevator stopped and we got out. I followed her to her room and stood there. She turned to me and looked at the floor for a moment. Then she spoke. "I want you to know something. I really enjoyed meeting you. And if I wasn't married and faithful to my husband, I'd invite you in." I told her I understood. Then, I said this: "I guess we'll never see each other again, huh? I had always wondered what it would be like to spend time with someone like you. It wasn't at all like I thought it would be. I really didn't know any woman could be as charming as you are. Tonight has bordered on being an episode of Fantasy Island. Well, good-bye to you, woman in the red dress. Have a good life. I know for a fact who the luckiest man in the world is. He's the one you're going home to. I'm a better man for having met you. See you later, doll."

And with that, I took her in my arms and kissed her with all the passion inherent in one who has climbed heights and overcome challenges. I released her, gave her my best "adios" salute, turned away and walked out of her life forever.

No, there wasn't any sex on my sojourn to the Big Apple, nothing even remotely resembling any kind of a romp with the ladies. But if there was ever any real romance in my life, it took place on a night in July 1992 with the full moon shining down on myself and the most beautiful woman in the world as I walked up Lexington Avenue with my arm around her waist. And it was . . . spectacular.

The only other experience I ever had with a beautiful woman took place later in the campaign. I had gone to a labor function and there were a lot of political types there. An aide to a prominent Alabama politician was also in attendance, and she had a date with him. She was a very politically motivated date—a very young, say early twenties, date.

She was talking to people around the room while her date was talking politics. Someone told her that a real political star was over there and pointed my way, so over she came. She introduced herself, as did I. I spent the next part of the evening talking to her about New York.

I did my best to impress this woman, so I put "war story" after "war story" upon her, taking her on a trip to the DNC from my vantage point. She seemed fascinated. She got physically closer to

J. R. HAMMOND

me with every story. She was twelve inches away from me, and she was dying for me to tell her more. So, I told her the "Inaugural Poem" I had written. It would be rude to tell you about it without telling it to you, so here it is.

FROM THE WORKERS

To work for a living, to hold down a job,
Should fill one with pride and esteem.
But the monied classes have tried to relegate workers,
To situations that only demean.

And belittle and pettify and lessen and stratify
Those whose labor makes this nation healthy and secure.
But a new wind blows fresh and pure.
And workers everywhere now know that their time has come to the fore.

And from Arkansas comes the key to the door,
And from Tennessee comes Albert Gore.

From Hope comes hope to the American clan
In the guise of a courageous Southern man,
Who will lead our nation to a higher place,
And working people of every race,

Americans all
Standing tall,

Will in unison say,
Thank you, President Clinton,
We needed that.

Powerful, huh? by the time I was finished with it, she was nose to nose with me.

I was face to face with another beautiful woman, her lips nearly touching mine, our eyes locked in a politically passionate glance as we stared deeply into each other's soul.

I had lived 41 years without interacting closely with a beautiful woman. Now I was reciting my poetry to the second one in three months. She was positively angelic and glowed with a youthful sensuality that was most alluring. It was as though the rest of the people had vanished, and we were all alone as we both stood there transfixed, motionless, and frozen in time. I started to kiss her.

But we were not alone. There was a room full of people, her

boyfriend was actually standing right behind me, and I could hear him talking. So good sense prevailed.

Instead of kissing her, I broke eye contact and told her how much I enjoyed meeting her. Her date called her name out, and she, too, was carried back into the room full of people. She smiled at me sweetly, and passed out of my life. I can tell you that never in my life did I want more to kiss a woman. Regret, thy name is missed opportunity with beautiful women.

Anyway, I spent 41 years without being in close contact with an actually beautiful woman, and then in a three-month period crossed paths with two of them. I even kissed one of them. How did I put it earlier? A typical working-class victory? Insignificant and irrelevant? Maybe so. But those were two really beautiful women, and for a few moments, I was a part of their world. One of them even promised not to forget me.

I've done worse.

⤷

A note from the Author to anyone who reads this book:

I wrote most of this book in 1992-1993. In January of 1994, I happened to meet a woman of such immense charm and beauty that I fell for her like a ton of bricks. In June of 1994 I was able to persuade her to become my wife. She is one neat lady, and while the Woman in Red and I strolling down Lexington Avenue was a sight to behold and will always be a most pleasant memory, the present Mrs. 'Working Man' Hammond is the woman I have waited for all my life. She is articulate, beautiful, warm, intelligent, and a GLB (Good-Looking-Babe) of the first magnitude. And I love her.

# CHAPTER 19

## Seven days without sleep makes one weak

You know, looking back on it now, it is a wonder I made it as well as I did, all things considered. I got about three hours sleep each night leading up to and all through the DNC. Since I am in my early forties, I can honestly say I'm not as young as I used to be.

The activities in New York were far more of a strain than ordinary coal mining due to the walking, the heat, and the flat-out pace I set for myself. I stayed busy all the time and never allowed myself to slow down for a minute.

While in fair health, I have the usual aches and pains anyone that works in the coal mines, or any heavy industry, is prone to have acquired during the years of hard bull-labor. Added to that is the fact that I was only eating a very light breakfast at 9 in the morning, and I went until 7 in the evening before I would dine in the hospitality suite. My fluid intake was reduced to whatever liquids I was able to get down between noon and 4 a.m in the hotel bar. (I drank water for the most part, because it was free. Anything else I may have quaffed came via volunteer contributions.) I would finally drift off to sleep around five, and was back up at seven to meet the day. Finally, in effect, I had been living on adrenaline since my election on June 2nd, five weeks earlier.

So it is little wonder that around noon, on July 15th, 1992, while standing on Broadway in the incredibly hot summer sun, I suddenly began to feel faint and knew that if I didn't get back to the hotel, I'd up and die.

They were having a big outdoor show that day featuring numbers and scenes from the best of the Broadway plays then running. There is usually between 1,300 and 1,400 feet of rock between myself and the sun, I am not a real "sun" person. I stick to the shade.

But I had gone there to Broadway to see some of what I was missing, some of what the rest of those there for the DNC were able to afford to go see.

I had found a place close and in front and was just waiting for the show to start when it hit me like a ton of bricks. I honestly thought I would pass out. I finally got over to a side street, staying in the shade as much as I could, and after a few anxious minutes, I hailed a big, yellow taxi to take me back to the hotel, cost be damned. After all, if I died from sunstroke, what good would $5 in my pocket do me?

I got into the back of the cab, and I waited for the driver to hold up the microphone so I could tell the dispatcher where I wanted to go and allow him to translate for me. Imagine my surprise when he said, "Where to, Mon?"

"Hey," I thought, "I'm saved!" At that moment I was most thankful for an English-speaking driver. I told him to get me to the Loew's Summit. As we rode, we talked. He said he had a wife and four children. He worked twelve hours a day, seven days a week, for straight time and tips. I asked him if the job held any fringe benefits, and he told me sometimes he got to meet nice people.

It occurred to me that he was one of us, a working stiff. He had his nose to the grindstone to feed his family. I asked him, "Do you have any health insurance?" He told me no. "What do you do if your wife or kids gets sick?" He said, "I just pray that they don't."

I told him, "Don't worry, pal. Come November, you and I and working people all over this nation will elect someone to the White House who will give you some medical insurance."

Once again, my experience was like a Frank Capra film. Not just any Capra film, but the definitive Capra masterpiece, *Mr. Smith Goes to Washington*.

A totally average guy—nonpolitical, good with kids—is suddenly propelled (due to forces outside the control of the Democratic Party) into a level of politics usually denied to working-class America. There I was, laid-off from work, not knowing how I was going to pay my house note, and telling this Haitian taxi driver that before long he would have insurance, thanks to President Clinton. I was acting like an official spokesman for Bill Clinton. It was good while it lasted.

I dragged myself inside to my room and collapsed on my bed. After a few minutes, I got up and took a cold shower and then

J. R. HAMMOND

afterwards collapsed on my bed. I dreamed I got out of bed and then collapsed again back on my bed. When I woke up, I had fallen off my bed.

I got back on my bed and took a nap. They say Edison took naps. I slept until the phone woke me up. It was WERC Radio AM in Birmingham, an "all-talk" station. They wanted to do an interview for the 12 o'clock news, live, the following day. I agreed, and I went back to sleep. On waking up, my second choice for relaxation was to go to the hotel's hot tub, so I did.

I was alone when I entered the hot tub, and I had the attendant turn the heat up as high as it would go. I was soon joined by another man, and it was none other than one of the black mayors from Alabama. It was a very Southern thing, a black mayor and a white voice of the American worker talking politics in a hot tub in a New York Hotel. Good luck, Mr. Mayor.

This time when I got back to my room and collapsed into my bed, I felt nearly human, and I was hungry to boot. I made myself get up, get dressed, and was in the process of heading down to the desk to see where the nearest "Burger World" was when I happened to cross paths with some of the gracious and sophisticated delegates from that fair and stalwart state of the Tarheels, North Carolina.

I tell you what. Those people from North Carolina were fabulous. Their Southern speech was a delight to my ears. I got along well with them. So it was no surprise to see them flagging me over to talk to them when I turned a corner and saw them across the lobby. They asked me if I wanted to go to a genuine North Carolina barbecue. My free food buzzer immediately went off, and I quickly accepted.

They fly this great barbecue in from anywhere in the country, and I think I heard someone say there was one thousand pounds of barbecued pork flown in for that party. It sure was tasty. They had all these games set up where you could win prizes. As I looked at the games, I noticed you couldn't lose! And the prizes included baseball hats, shirts, and socks, and all of them had cigarette company brand names on them. (I think the tobacco companies had sprung for the barbecue, also.) This is how the U.S. government works. Big companies buy barbecue, for some people, and these people think kindly of them for it. It's too bad working people can't afford to buy barbecue for their leaders.

Then, after I was through eating, this beautiful, older woman from North Carolina came over and we talked, and she told me I was now an honorary North Carolinian, and I was proud of it. She had seen me on stage opening night and just wanted to tell me hello and thanks for a job well done. It was a neat thing to have someone from another part of the country who appreciated you. I really liked those Carolina people.

I went back to my room and rested until 3 p.m., and then I got up and went down to the lobby to see what was going on. This turned out to be a terrible mistake, for at 3:05 p.m. NBC News called and wanted to interview me that night. If I had gotten that phone call, I probably would not be writing this now, as some movie maker would have already made a film about me. Blown opportunities have a way of haunting you.

So I was in the lobby, hanging out in the bar because it took up most of the lobby, and I could get free water there, when I made my second mistake of the day. Only this one hurt me then, not later. Despite the heat, the humidity, and my general fatigue, I decided to walk the 17 blocks from my hotel to Madison Square Garden. I honestly didn't know that New York blocks were five times longer than Birmingham blocks. I started walking, and I walked, and walked, and I began to feel ill again. It took me over half an hour of walking—and I mean hard walking—to get there. By the time I finally got there I was gone. Exhausted, hot, sweaty, you name it, I felt it. I made my way inside and headed right for the hospitality suite. I just decided to rest there for a while and have dinner. I noticed the crowd to be bigger that night, but there were county-level officials there that night instead of the big cats I was used to. Some of them joined me in the booth where I was sitting since there were no empty tables.

By and by, I headed back to the main floor and found a seat in the back of the delegation. I just wanted to sit quietly and be left alone. The DNC was gaveled into session, and I promptly went to sleep. I would sit there asleep for a few minutes, wake up and look around, and then I would pass out again. I was just plumb give out.

Around 10 p.m., somebody tapped me on the shoulder and asked me if I was all right. It took. I felt much better. Anybody that can sleep upright in a chair on the floor of the DNC while, in addition to the normal chaos, there are spontaneous demonstrations by radical supporters of a losing candidate shaking you and waking you up to tell you they are for homosexual rights, is really tired. One good way to turn someone against your cause is to wake them up to tell them about it. I shook the cobwebs out of my head and decided the best way to get back to full speed would be to wander around some, so away I went.

I walked around the Garden and checked the place out, that night. I wandered over towards the back of the building, checking out all those unfortunate states that did not have front row seats. Viewed from the back of Madison Square, the stage was a very long distance away. I tried to meet as many delegates from other states as I could, particularly of the female persuasion.

I noticed a commotion going on down in the Arkansas section, and I remembered Governor Clinton was to make an appearance. I had just made it back to the stage when a roar went up from the crowd. Governor Bill Clinton was about to go up to the stage and be officially recognized by the convention. As he made his way towards the podium, millions of pieces of blue glitter were dropped from the ceiling and fell like rain. It was the driest, most colorful blizzard I had ever been in.

This was the high point of Wednesday night, and we adjourned to the hotel. There was a party of the highest caliber going on that night with a live band and everything. As I celebrated along with everybody else, I thought about the fact that my time as something other than an average guy was about over. I wanted a special keepsake of the Working Man in NYC.

I knew that I was 24 hours away from returning to normal life. I had the two tapes of my poetry, and the two interviews I had done, but I wanted something different. I asked the guitarist of the band if I could play his guitar and sing a song. He asked me if I could play, and I said let's see. I did a song I wrote about a woman who left me. It is a poignant story about a man's surprising encounter with the truth. It's a song to remember. It carries a basic G-C-E minor musical signature. I have a tape of the song I played, and it sure is amusing. Here it is.

IF I ONLY KNEW

Oh, I knew when you left me
I would be blue.

Yes, I knew when you left me,
It would make me blue.

I knew when you left me
I would be blue.

But if I,
Only knew,
Just how happy,
You made me,
When you left me,
I would have helped you pack your clothes months ago,
Then I would have shown you to the door,
And gassed up the car for you.
If I only knew.

Well, the song went over big, and the crowd at the hotel bar was rockin' with American democracy in action. I hung around until everybody else went to bed, and I turned in at my usual 4 a.m.

The final day awaited me. At least I would have a good view of the stage from the front row seats of the Alabama delegation. Turned out, I had to stand up all during the Clinton acceptance speech. Turned out, I wasn't even going to be in the Alabama delegate area during the speech.

Fate was to write another chapter. Fate had elevated me to the opening night ceremony. What could fate have in store for me on closing night? Fate was dealing the cards, and I was catching aces.

# CHAPTER 20

## President Clinton and the Working Man

I t was the morning of the last day of the 1992 DNC. As usual, I awoke at 7 a.m., showered, did my best to clear my head, and headed off to get my credentials for my last day in politics. At least at the time, I thought it was. I put on my funeral suit and headed up to the penthouse. One morning, the news crew from the McNeil-Lehrer News Hour was there because they said we were the most interesting delegation. They interviewed me, but because I had not been there for the 1988 Convention, they left me out of the show. Pity.

Senator Richard Shelby was there that morning, so I met him for the first time. Like I said earlier, Senator Howell Heflin had warmed up to me and acted very friendly towards me, and his wife is a true Southern belle. I think she was the nicest person I met, as far as the big wheels go. I got up and made a little speech to the rest of the delegation, thanking them for their hospitality. After getting our delegate passes for the final night of the DNC, everyone went out for one last day in New York.

I ended up having a burger and fries lunch at the Star Deli as the guest of then Congressman Claude Harris. When's the last time a congressman bought you lunch, huh? I really liked him. He is missed in Congress.

I decided to go to the hotel hot tub again and try to get this old body in shape for one last night of the DNC. As I was relaxing in the tub, another black guy came in and joined me. He told me his name was Virgil, and he worked for Governor Mario Cuomo. I told him all about myself being the Working Man, and how the Democratic Party should use me as a selling point because there was nobody in the Republican Party like me, and that meant only in the Democratic Party could an average American like myself be sitting there in a hot tub talking politics with an aide to the Governor of New York. He was impressed to the point of telling me that he was a friend of Ron Brown, and he would personally send him a letter about me and send me a copy of it.

He told me to leave my address with the hotel staff, and I would be hearing from him. As you may have guessed, I'm still waiting to hear from Virgil.

I arrived back to my room just in time for the noon live radio interview. It lasted ten minutes. Listeners could tell I was tired, because I said I was tired. But I told them I could feel the magic in the air, and that come November, look out Republicans, 'cause we are going to win. It was a good interview, and when I signed off, I said, "God bless America," and I felt very sincere in being a part of this campaign.

As I sat there looking at the phone I had just spoken into, I began to think of all that had happened to me in the short span of six days. My election under the name 'Working Man' Hammond was a wonderment of the first magnitude, and the ensuing media interest had given me a chance to speak for the other 200 million working-class people. I always wanted to do that.

And people high up in the future Clinton administration told me that I was in like Flynn, and would be after the election also. I was a hit in the Alabama delegation. I had been on stage in front of nationwide television, had been interviewed by two nationwide television crews, and I was going to be on the front row that night for the biggest show on Earth.

A feeling of awe came over me. Although I am not the most religious man around, I always have believed in God. It hit me like a tidal wave just how generous He had been to me, one of the multitude. During all the time I had spent in New York at the Convention, I had met a lot of delegates from all the other states, but I had not met anybody else there who was an honest-to-God blue-collar person like me.

I was a part of that 80 percent of Americans who are not involved in politics and are never allowed to be a part of the process. I had been in politics for 43 days, and the *Birmingham News* identified me as a "minor celebrity" at the convention. By this point, I personally had met more politically powerful people than probably any other rank and file American.

I had experienced the food, the parties, and four hours with the most beautiful, charming, and intelligent woman in the history of mankind; and yet basically, I was the same man I had been 44 days earlier.

And then.....

And then I realized that I could never be the same man I had been before. I knew that I could never have done what I had without God's help. I could not have become a spokesman for the American worker without God's help. I could not have faced the cameras and the press without divine intervention. I felt humble in the eyes of the Lord as I never had before.

I looked up at the ceiling, out the window into the sky, and I looked into myself. I fell on my knees and told the Lord thanks. I said, "Lord, I know I'm not worthy of this great honor you have bestowed on me. I know that I am not the kind of man worthy of one-tenth of the experiences I've had this last week. I know you must have had some plan for me, or you would not have let me be a part of this. I will be a better man, Lord, and whatever the future holds for me, I will face it unafraid. I know I'm not worthy, Lord, but I humbly thank you."

I said, "Amen," got up off the floor, and sat down on the bed. I was in the process of wiping my eyes and regaining my composure when the phone rang. I looked towards the sky and said aloud and jokingly, even though I assume God can hear you think, "Well, Lord, I guess this is Clinton calling to invite me to dinner." You can say stuff like this when you're alone, you know, without being looked at funny.

"Hello, this is the Working Man."

The voice on the line was that of my Clinton delegate coordinator, Mr. Glen Rushing.

"Working Man! How are you?"

Rather than tell him I had just had a religious experience, I just said I was doing fine and looking forward to tonight.

What he told me next was this: "Working Man, Governor Clinton knows how hard you've worked this week, but he has one more job for you. He wants you to join him on stage tonight after his acceptance speech and represent the working people of America. He wants the American workers to know that they are a part of things now and will be after he is elected. Will you do it?"

Naturally, I agreed, and then he said, "One more thing, Working Man, don't tell anyone and it'll be a big surprise." I knew that was true because I was very surprised myself. He told me he had to go, so I thanked him and said good-bye.

As I sat there in stunned silence, I again looked up towards the heavens and marveled at the mysterious ways of the Lord. I said in my most humble voice, "Boy, when you send someone a message, you don't fool around, do you?"

Now maybe I was just exhausted, maybe it was just a coincidence, and maybe I took a series of unrelated events and—due to my emotional condition, which at that moment was highly suggestive to say the least—arrived at the mistaken conclusion that for some reason God had taken an active role in my life. I cannot deny the possibility that it just happened because it happened. But in that room on that July afternoon, it was as close to a miracle as I can imagine. First, I got down on my knees and thanked God for my being elected a delegate, for being a real part of the 1992 DNC, and for giving me the poise and confidence to carry myself in a manner befitting a representative of the American workers. I told Him I knew I was not worthy, but I would be a better man and would handle whatever else he sent my way. And the moment I said, "Amen," the phone rang and I was told that our next President wanted me on stage with him to represent the American workers. You may think it was coincidence, but you weren't in that room with me. It was a life-changing experience, and one for the better.

Have you ever had a big secret you were not supposed to tell? In a way, I was just given one. I decided to cool it until I left, so I didn't cross paths with anyone that afternoon before I left for the Garden. The people I talked to on the bus got only routine chatter out of me that day.

When I got to the Convention hall, it was still a couple of hours to kickoff, so I went several places inside. I went to NBC to see if they still wanted to talk to me, and they didn't. I went by and spoke to Peter Jennings of ABC again and tried to have my photo made with him, and of course my flash didn't work and the picture didn't take. I went over to the Clinton trailers under the left-hand seats.

I sent word in to my delegate coordinator, Glen Rushing, that the Working Man was there to see him. Not only did he come out, but a dozen or so of his youthful coworkers came out with him. They all greeted me very warmly, and in a group they went to the stage so that I could take photos of them in front of the dais with all the colorful stage decorations in the picture. They also took some pictures with me in there with them. After all, they loved me in Little Rock.

I spent the rest of the afternoon wandering around, trying to hide my excitement and connect up with a woman who might be interested in a coal miner turned Voice of the American Worker. By my count I ended up 0 for 27 all told, but by this last afternoon of the Convention I had reached only 23. Hey, I was polite, subtle for the most part, and other than one girl from North Carolina who seemed shocked, they all handled my overtures in a most dignified manner. If there is a more beautiful creation than woman, I have yet to cast eyes on it.

A friend I had made from the North Carolina delegation, an alternate delegate, crossed paths with me in my wanderings that afternoon. He was an alternate, and as such had no floor pass that night, and he told me the North Carolina delegation seating was full up, and could I help?

"Oh, but yes," I replied, and sat him down next to me in the Alabama section. He had his credentials turned around backwards so security wouldn't throw him out. It was so crowded that seats were at a premium everywhere in the hall. Several Alabama delegates had no place to sit, including some very powerful members of the Alabama crew, such as one of the chief black leaders in Alabama, one of our Congressmen, and a few others. It was comical in a way, but there were so many chairless folks that the seat my North Carolina friend occupied wouldn't have made much difference even if he had gotten up. Around 7 p.m. my pal and I were offered passes to the hospitality suite, which was a ploy to get our seats then. I politely declined. So I was able to pay back North Carolina for its gracious hospitality.

At one point we got thirsty, so I had Carolina hold our seats while I headed for the Coke machine. I spoke to the workers having lunch in their break room one last time, and they wished me well. I had two ice-cold canned Cokes in hand as I was walking down the stairs back towards the convention floor.

I noticed a small herd of what I call suit-boys, Ivy-League types in their twenties, sporting fancy clothes and sharp haircuts. They were types that were used to pushing around the little guys like myself, guys that think they know it all—suit-boys with a natural arrogance that they exude from every pore. They were loudly talking politics so everyone within earshot would know they were the Ivy-League suit-boys that would serve in the administration once Clinton went into the White House. As I passed them, the leader suit-boy saw me with the two Cokes. He reached out and grabbed my arm, then told me this, "Hey, I'll give you $5 for one of those."

This stopped me in my tracks. I looked at him and thought of how I had been around all these people with money and how they had an air of invincibility about them. Then I realized he was trying to get the Coke because he thought I would jump at the money. He probably thought I was a stage hand or something. I had to respond in the correct manner: "Turn loose of my arm. Thank you." He turned loose of my arm, and waited for his Coke.

I said, "If you had asked me for it, I would have given it to you. If you had asked me how to get to the drink machine, I would have shown you there myself. But you don't have enough money to buy one of these Cokes. Excuse me." I left them there gawking at each other.

I made my way back to my seat, and gave my pal his Coke. I said, "Drink that thing slow. It cost me $5." He and I drank our Cokes merrily.

As I sat there knowing that in a very few minutes I would be meeting the next President on stage at the DNC in front of another nationwide audience, I decided the shirt I had on was all wrong. I went out to one of the many retailers in the hallway and purchased a white cotton Clinton-Gore tee-shirt to wear while being seen by the whole country. It seemed like a good idea at the time. At this late date, $15 for a clean shirt seemed like a bargain. And in the tee-shirt I did stick out from the others on stage that night.

Finally, I got a call to come to the trailers that the Clinton people used as headquarters to prepare for the trip through security and to the back of the stage.

I ended up acting as a cowhand, rounding up those 21 delegates into one group as they would come drifting back to the meeting place. There was a lot going on back there.

Senator Pat Moynihan of New York came by with a big bag of buttons with "Potatoe" on them. (You remember the Dan Quayle spelling incident.) He was giving them out, so I went over, looked him in the face, and said, "Give me one, Senator!" He looked me dead in the eyes, turned his nose up at me and walked away. Thanks a lot, pal. I like you, too. Ex-candidate for President Paul Tsongas came by, and spoke to one of the guys going on stage with me.

This man is a hair cutter from Pennsylvania, and an African-American, and a unique individual. He had it even worse than I did during the Monday night ceremony because they got his name mixed up with someone else. Sonny, I hope to see you again someday. You can trim my hair. That's a joke.

Tsongas told Sonny he had a lot of buttons on. He did, too. But so did I. In fact, while I was in the restroom adjusting my buttons, one of those Ivy-League types told me a person should never wear more than three buttons.

I said, "Who asked you?" Some people . . .

Once we were all rounded up, we went through many layers of security, until we found ourselves in a small room. There was a television set tuned to the convention, and Al Gore was coming on stage. I must admit, the theme of "It's time for them to go" played as well as any speech in my memory.

I looked around the room at the faces of my compatriots as they too listened to the Tennessean drive home his main message. I had a seat on a desk, and while it was not the most comfortable, it had to be the most dramatic desk job I ever held down. As the hands on the clock spun towards my appointment with the closing night ceremonies, I was tempted to pinch myself as a reality check. The heat and the closeness of the small office I shared with 21 other delegates, in addition to the people who worked there, was evidence a plenty that I was just where I seemed to be.

When Al Gore left the stage, it was time for us to move to the back of the stage. Our leader was a top aide to Frank Greer, the man who headed up Bill Clinton's '92 campaign media effort. She was as beautiful as she was sharp, and believe you me, she was sharp as a tack. We assembled at the base of the stairs leading up to the rear of the stage, and after one more secret service checkpoint, we, the 21 diverse individuals from all across the nation, climbed the stairs that led to the stage level (except for the guy in the wheelchair, who rode a small elevator).

We were behind that huge wall of televisions at the back of the stage. This was a level reserved for those people who were so high up in the scheme of things as to be absolutely no threat to the next President. While there were agents up in the seats behind the stage, there were none in our group, and none too close to us.

We were given our instructions, and I was told to stand right in front of Bill Clinton, one level down. It sure sounded good to me. We were to be the first group to go on after Bill Clinton had finished his speech and was joined by his family. Unfortunately, the plan was changed, and all the big cats in the Democratic Party were to be around him, and we were supposed to make room for them to go down to the bottom level. As the instructions were being told to us, a huge, staggering, roar of applause burst forth from the audience, and we knew that our man Bill was taking the stage for his acceptance speech. And so it began.

I wandered around to the edge of the stage and looked out. It was a real sight to behold for this average American boy gone to the big city. I shook my head in wonderment. I realized the significance of my situation, to be a truly non-political person, and not even active in the Democratic Party, being given the first-hand political experiences I was having. And now being personally chosen by the campaign of the next President to go on stage with him as a representative of my fellow working Americans.

I wondered if perhaps I should use the opportunity to make a political statement, to communicate to the audience that one of the little people who keeps this great and beautiful nation of ours going was standing up for them on the stage of the Democratic National Convention. But that is not the style of the American workers. President Nixon used to call us the "silent majority," and in one sense he was correct. Making a living through long hours and hard work and raising a family takes too many hours a day, too many days a week, and too many weeks a year to allow us the luxury of much direct political involvement. We stand on the sidelines watching, not asking for much, just wanting a nod in our direction to let us know we are not forgotten.

But tonight, the leadership of the Democratic Party and the next President of the United States of America would not only nod to us, but by golly, would meet one of us face-to-face.

As Clinton's acceptance speech drew towards its conclusion, all of the National Democratic Party leadership—the Senators, Governors, Paul Tsongas, and others—were assembled on the stairwell leading up to the stage. As I looked over at the faces of those at the top of the stairs, I saw New York City Mayor David Dinkins and New York Governor Mario Cuomo on the top step. So, considering the great time I had had in their city and state, I wanted to personally thank them.

J. R. HAMMOND

I surprised the mayor when I walked over and tapped him on the shoulder. He turned around and I said, "Great city, pal. You did really good. I'll come back again one day." Governor Cuomo then turned around, so I reached out and shook his hand and said hello to him, also. Too bad Virgil wasn't around. I was close enough to actually look down the stairwell, and at the bottom of the stairs was Jesse Jackson. I sort of yelled out, "Hey Jesse," to him. And then, this blonde lady who had her back to me turned around and looked me in the face.

She was the wife of Paul Michael Glaser, who starred on the TV show Starsky and Hutch. She had given a speech on AIDS earlier in the Convention. She had contracted the disease through a blood transfusion, and told us of her personal battle with the scourge of mankind. She came across as a courageous and classy lady.

I am afraid of this disease, just like everybody else with good sense. I had never been around anyone with it, and had never wanted to be around anyone with it, either. But I had read the reports, and it is supposed to be a fact that casual contact is safe. While she and I come from vastly different worlds, during her presentation to the convention I felt her anguish, her pain, and her isolation. I was moved into action.

Her hand was ahold of the railing that went around the top of the stairwell. I walked over and placed my hand atop hers. I squeezed it gently, and when she turned to face me with a most puzzled look in her eye, I told her, "Have courage, ma'am. My daughter and I will pray for you. You are not alone." She nodded, gave as best a smile as someone in her situation can give, and told me "thank you."

The signal was given; get ready to go on. I lined up with the others and got set. I could see on the monitors that Clinton and Gore, along with their families, were already in the center of the stage. We were told our cue to go was the start of the music. I wondered what they would play.

I've always loved Fleetwood Mac. Stevie Nix is the most beautiful and graceful woman ever to grace the stage at a rock concert. When the strains of "Don't Stop Thinking About Tomorrow" began to fill the Garden, I began to move to the beat.

Then, it was go, go, go, and we headed out towards the stage. As I walked out on the stage with the future first and second families, I decided against going over and kissing Hilary and Tipper, and then hugging the necks of Bill and Al, although by not doing so I cost myself a spot on the Letterman and Leno shows. Instead, I quickly headed over to the left side of the stage, directly in front of the Alabama delegation. As I stood over them, looking down at them, I looked into the faces of those I had come to know during the previous week. They responded in a most uproarious show of approval. While the other 49 states and sundry territories were at that moment cheering Clinton and Gore, the Alabama gang was saluting me. It was better than sex, at least from what I remembered of sex, anyway.

The rest of the national Democratic leadership and friends were now filling the stage, and I was crowded down further towards the bottom levels of the stage until I was on the bottom rung. Small U.S. flags were given out to the crowd, and this nice woman who was next to the railing that kept the crowd off the stage was leaning over the railing and waving one of these flags. I was close enough to ask her if I could have her flag to wave, and she gave it to me. Thank you, ma'am, wherever you are.

So, for the next 20 minutes or so, I stood on the bottom rung of the stage waving my flag and clapping. It was the winding down period for the 1992 DNC. It had been some kind of a week, and I think everyone felt it.

The crowd began to thin onstage, as the lesser figures began to exit, leaving Bill and Al to finish it off. I began to make my way back towards the upper levels, and a path to Al Gore appeared. I made my way through the $1,000 suits until I was within handshaking distance. I extended my right hand towards Gore, and he did the same. As we shook, I nodded and said, "Good show." He smiled at me and said, "Thanks." Then my California friend Ron Gillis and I made it back to the top level of the stage, and we watched from six feet away as Bill Clinton faced a crowd of people around him. The mob suddenly split, and there was a clear path to the next President of the United States of America.

I walked up to the future President Clinton, and stood toe-to-toe with the man from Hope. We both extended our right hands, and as we began to shake hands, I spoke to him. "Governor Clinton, my name is J. R. 'Working Man' Hammond, and I'm a coal miner from Woodstock, Alabama. You don't have to worry about Alabama's nine electoral votes, sir. If I have to go to all 67 counties and carry the state for you by myself, Alabama's votes will be yours."

He nodded and replied, "Well, I sure need them. Thanks."

*There I am, amidst the pandemonium following the acceptance speech,
and a few minutes before I shook hands with the next President.*

I told him it was nice meeting him, and he said, "Me, too," and
the crowd began to form around him again, so I told him good-bye,
and we parted company. That was my face-to-face meeting with Bill
Clinton, on stage there at Madison Square Garden around 11:45
p.m. on July 16th, 1992.

I walked back over to my pal Ron, and we stood there and talked as the candidates left the stage.

We were just about the only people left on stage when a man approached us. He spoke to me.

" 'Working Man' Hammond, you don't know me, but I know you. I'm Frank Greer, and I'm the one who picked you to be up here. You've done a fine job." His aide, Kara Kelly, was with him, and she, too, congratulated me. He gave me his business card, and they left. Eventually, Ron and I were escorted off the stage, and out into the night. I walked him back to his bus, and waved good-bye. He is a good guy.

I got on my own bus and found a seat in the rear. There was no one next to me. At that moment, Mary Steenburgen—the movie star—boarded the bus. She walked past me to sit next to a woman, so I said drat! I was glad to at least be this close to her on the final night. She did sit about six rows back of the Alabama delegation all during the DNC, so I was in close proximity to her, anyway, and I have two snapshots that show both of us side by side. But I never actually spoke to her. Too bad.

But the woman seated next to her did something Mary didn't like, and she came out of the seat saying how rude the woman was, and came over and sat down next to me. What's a Working Man to do? I just wanted to say hello.

I carefully thought out the next sequence of events, and came up with this: I turned to her, and in a very respectful way said "Ma'am, I do not mean to invade your privacy, but I am a single parent raising my 16-year-old daughter, Elesha, and she is a big fan of yours. Would you please give me an autograph for her?" She said, "Of course," and did. We chatted the rest of the ride. She has daughters herself, so we spoke about the kids, and she told me what a good friend of hers Bill Clinton was. We shook hands as she left the bus. She is as classy as she is beautiful.

Back at the hotel, they were having a going-away party for the delegations from Alabama, Kansas, and North Carolina. They were giving as door prizes the decorations that had been up during the week. I didn't win one, but the Alabama delegation had a red donkey cutout as a gift for me, signed by all the Alabama people there that night. I have it on the wall of my mobile home. It was very flattering.

The party went on until about 4 a.m., and then it broke up. I figured since I had hardly slept in a week, one more night wouldn't hurt. I wandered down to the Colorado HQ, and it was like a wake. I then went over to the Arkansas HQ, and hung out there until fatigue forced me out into the street and back towards my room and my departure from New York.

As I walked up Lexington Avenue, intense feelings came over me. I thought of the things I had done during the last week, the people I had met, and what I had tried to do for the American worker. I felt as though I had carried myself about as well as any man or woman could have under the circumstances. As far as I could tell, no other delegate had been able to be more of a symbol of blue-collar Americans at the Democratic National Convention.

I wasn't even in politics, yet I had been told by aides to our next President that I was one of them, and after the election I would have input and access to the White House.

I had met and talked to the next President of the U.S.A. face to face, with no one around us. It was just him and me, for a minute there.

And while I still had the campaign to go, I was saddened to think that this particular great adventure into national politics was over. In a few hours I would be on my plane back to Birmingham, and once off the plane, I would no longer be the Voice of the American worker. As reality crept back into my life, I made my way up to my room.

I gave the order for a 7 a.m. wake-up call, which by my bleary-eyed look at my watch was about one hour away. Fully dressed, and dead tired, I collapsed on my bed. The phone rang, I answered it and was told it was time to get ready to check out of the hotel, and then check out of New York City.

I didn't bother to actually pack all my keepsakes; I just threw everything into my suit bag, stuffed my clothing into my suitcase, and headed down to the lobby. There we boarded a bus to carry us out to the airport. I really began to feel the strain. My luggage weighed a ton, as did my legs, arms, and the rest of my body. I was beginning to feel really sick.

I had always had somewhat of a fear of flying, but that morning I discovered a cure for it. The way to get over your fear of flying is to feel so bad that the idea of the plane crashing doesn't sound all that bad. I felt so bad that morning that I would have had to have gotten better to die.

Mercifully, the plane took off and I went to sleep. An hour later,

I was awakened by the stewardess with a lunch tray. I was in total misery. My head felt like it was coming off. Then I tried to remember the last time I had eaten. The best I could figure, it was some time Wednesday evening. No wonder I was sick, as this was Friday afternoon. You hear a lot of jokes about airplane food, and I don't travel enough to be able to tell you really just how it is. But that turkey sandwich and bowl of corn chowder brought me back to life. By the time I got back to Birmingham, I was feeling much better. Sharing the flight with me was Donald Langham, another Alabama labor leader. He's another fine leader I'm proud to know.

It is so good to come back home. As I disembarked from the plane, and walked the corridor leading from the plane to the terminal, I saw a petite, blonde, teenaged girl waiting for her father to come home from the big city. I grabbed her and gave her a hug. I also gave her the red, white, and blue donkey I had in my lap all the way back from N.Y.C. She named him Frederick. She wrote a story about him. He was well behaved on the trip home.

Well, it was over. I could hardly speak, and I was totally exhausted and unemployed. I made it to my home (Elesha drove.) And after seeing her off for a weekend trip to her mom's, I laid down on the couch to rest. But before I went to sleep, I made one phone call.

"Hello there, Dollface. This is J. R. Yes, I know I don't sound like myself, but I'll be okay in a few days. How's about you coming over here and giving me some of that TLC, baby. Yeah, tonight. Sure, you're safe. Well, the thought did cross my mind. No, that is not all I'm interested in. Well, okay, maybe later. Not in this lifetime? Hello? Hello?"

Rats.

J. R. HAMMOND

# 4

## The Campaign

# CHAPTER 21

## Welcome Back to Reality/My Political Career
## Lives on a While Longer

After spending one more lonely Friday night, I began to recover from the rigors of my New York adventure. My voice came back, and I decided to do what I could for the cause. Since everything I had done so far I had done pretty much on my own, I called the three top television stations in Birmingham and arranged interviews with each.

The first aired on the Saturday evening 5 p.m. news on Channel 6 (WBRC-TV, ABC), and in it I told how this was a new Democratic Party, and that my job was to get out the word that there was no way we could lose with the stuff we use. It went off well. It was recorded and edited, but it was okay.

I did another recorded and edited interview for the Sunday evening 5 p.m. news on Channel 13 (WVTM-TV, NBC). In this one, I told how after 12 years of Republican rule, the economy was in a shambles. This interview, too, was okay.

But my favorite interview of that weekend was a live broadcast I did for the July 18, 1992, 10 p.m. news at Channel 42 (WBMG, CBS).

I was attending a party very close to the television station, and it was a kick to be able to tell folks that I had to leave early because I had a live TV interview at 10 p.m. In it I came across as a true grassroots American who had gone above and beyond the call of duty to do something for the working class. I told the interviewers about the taxi driver to whom I had promised the Democrats would work to bring relief from the crisis of no health insurance. The two anchor people told me I was an inspiration to working people everywhere.

Since it was Saturday night, and still early, I went to meet a friend of mine at a local bar. As I was walking along the centrally located bar through a crowd of people, I stopped to get a drink—a kind of celebratory toast to a good interview. The guy next to me glanced

J. R. HAMMOND

over, then turned away, then did the classic double take, jumped off his bar stool and exclaimed, "I just saw you on television! You were great! I want to shake your hand!" So I let him buy me another drink, swapped a few war stories, and left. This kind of reaction happened often, which shows that average people like it when one of their own has a chance to speak out.

On Thursday, July 16, 1992, I had spent four hours getting backstage for my 45 minutes onstage with Bill and Al and the rest of the Big Cats. On Monday, July 20, 1992, I spent four hours waiting to sign up for my $160 a week unemployment compensation check. Talk about a sudden return to reality. I actually gave an interview to Alabama Public Radio from the pay phone outside the employment office.

I gave one more speech to my local on July 25, 1992, telling about my trip to the DNC, and as of that day, I decided my career in politics was over. But fate has a way of playing tricks on you.

Things rocked on for the next few weeks. I was still laid-off and not really planning on anything else as far as Campaign '92 went. The people I worked with wanted some Clinton stickers and the like, so I kept in touch with Alabama Democratic Party HQ. They told me it would be mid-August before the materials would arrive. So, on August 12, 1992, I phoned to check on things and they told me to come by, they had some signs and bumper stickers.

I drove to the Alabama Democratic Party Headquarters in Birmingham and was in the process of getting an armload of stickers and signs when I was summoned to the office of Al LaPierre, second-in-command of the Alabama Democratic Party structure. I couldn't guess why he wanted to see me.

Another person was there, the chairman of the Walker County Democratic Party. It seems they were having a County Executive Board meeting that Saturday in Jasper, Alabama (about 50 miles northwest of Birmingham), and he wanted a speaker for the meeting to give them a report of the DNC. Since I was there at the same time the Country Chairman was there, I was elected.

Well, I had to do the speech in two days, and I didn't really know what I was going to say. So I sat down at my daughter's Smith-Corona and began. I wanted to write something that would stir the soul, that would communicate to the audience the passion and fire I felt there in NYC at the DNC, that was so good that when I finished there would be thunderous applause and the people would rise up spontaneously and declare to the world that this was the greatest speech ever written, and then go out door-to-door and canvass for the Clinton-Gore ticket. Yeah, and I was going to find a cure for cancer, bring on world peace, and grow my hair back, all at the same time.

So, I wrote. By 1 a.m Friday I had a rough draft, and by Friday evening I was finished. Late that night, I called my old friend Pete Troup (I told you I would work you into the book somehow) and put it on him. He said it was great. I prepared for the 80-mile drive to Jasper the next day, and was ready to give it my best shot. A thought occurred to me. Was I once again the Voice of the American Worker? No, one speech did not a Voice of the American Worker make. Oh well, at least it would be something new. New experiences and myself—in the summer of '92—had become frequent flyers on the same airline, the Working Man Express.

I got to the courthouse and found the room in which I was supposed to give my speech. I watched the room fill with Walker County Democrats, and did my best to look and act like a cool customer, which in actuality I had become.

I listened to the preliminaries, and then I was introduced to those in attendance. I approached the podium with a feeling of excitement and readiness. I stood behind the podium, cleared my head of all nervousness and told them these words that I had written the day before.

Good morning. My name is J. R. Hammond, but you may have heard of me by the name "Working Man" Hammond, delegate to the Democratic National Convention from the 7th Congressional District. I have been a coal miner for 18 years, and I am a full-time single parent to my teenage daughter, Elesha. I have not been involved in politics before, but with the disastrous elections of 1980, 1984, and 1988 to look back at, and the prospect of four more years of Republican mismanagement to look forward to, I knew I had to make an effort to bring my Party back to the middle of the road. I had the idea that if I could run under a name that would signify who I was and what I stood for, if I could get the voters to identify with me, then I could win a delegate spot to the DNC and be a true representative of the great forgotten majority, the working people of this great and beautiful nation.

I have heard that there is nothing as powerful as an idea whose time has come, and so, much to the surprise of many, I was elected delegate to the 1992 DNC.

When Governor Clinton said they had a genuine grass-roots

Democrat at the convention, they honored me and made me part of the opening night ceremonies. As I stood in the middle of the stage there in Madison Square Garden and fellow Democrats from all over the country applauded and saluted me, I felt a thrill of monumental proportions. I knew that nothing would ever even come close to this again.

I enjoyed the next two days of the DNC, and looked forward to watching Governor Clinton's acceptance speech from the Convention floor. Alabama had front row seats, and we had as good a view of things as anyone there.

Then around 1 p.m. Thursday afternoon, the phone rang. It was a Clinton staff member calling. I had been dealing with him, discussing the role of the American worker in the upcoming campaign and the ensuing Clinton Presidency. He told me that Governor Clinton knew how hard I had worked that week but that he had one more job for me. Would I join him on stage that night after his acceptance speech to represent the working people to New York to do just that. He then asked me not to tell anyone so it would be a surprise. I had to agree with him. I was surprised myself.

I'm just a coal miner, just a working person who made an effort to bring the Democratic Party back to a more moderate direction, just an average guy with an idea whose time had come, yet I was going to share the stage with the next President of the United States of America. And I couldn't tell anyone about it. I did smile a lot that day.

I slipped away from the delegation around 8:00, and by 11:00 I was behind that big wall of televisions at the back of the stage, having made my way through countless though necessary layers of secret service agents. As I watched and listened to Governor Clinton's message of moderation and healing for this nation I became aware of the unique position I found myself in.

How many ordinary working people had ever been given such an honor? Had anyone from grassroots America ever been asked to share in such a moment as this? Then, it was time to go on. As I came out from behind that big wall of televisions I headed over to the left side of the stage. I reached the edge I looked over and was face-to-face with the Alabama delegation. I saw them cheering and waving at me and giving me the thumbs-up, and then I saw Jasper's own State Senator Bob Wilson, and he gave me two thumbs-up and it was the best.

I am now a driven man, with only two things in my life: Taking care of my daughter, Elesha, and working for the election of Bill Clinton.

This is the most critical election since 1932, and this is the finest ticket we have fielded since Roosevelt-Truman in 1944. It is up to us, the grass roots of the Democratic Party, to carry the message that this is a new Democratic Party with direction based on our Southern traditions of moderation and away from the losing liberal platforms of the eighties.

I know we can win. I know we must win. Alabama is a key state.

After twenty minutes on the stage, I made my way over and shook Al Gore's hand. I turned, and then walked up to Bill Clinton. I looked him right in the eye and said "Governor Clinton, if I have to go to all 67 counties and carry the state for you by myself, Alabama's votes will be yours." He smiled and said "thanks, I need them."

Let us work together to get Bill Clinton what I promised him, Alabama's nine electoral votes. Thank you and God bless you.


As I walked away there was silence at first, and then much and vigorous applause. I had a very good feeling when I sat back down, and knew I had given it my best.

The county chairman then got up to introduce the other guest for that meeting, a Mr. Jeff Deroen. Turns out he was the Alabama State Field Representative for the Clinton campaign, sent here directly from Little Rock. He got up and introduced himself, and asked if there were any questions or comments. One of the Walker county Executive Board members stood up and said, "Yes, I've got something to say."

"You should take Working Man all over the country because that is the best speech I've ever heard!"

He looked over at me, nodded in my direction, and said yes, he was planning on meeting with me and discussing plans for the future. This was news to me.

As the meeting broke up, he came by and introduced himself and asked me if I could come by State Headquarters that evening on my way back through Birmingham. I said, "Sure, I'll see you after a while."

I had written a poem for Bill Clinton, and it was my plan to ask him if I could read it at the State Headquarters Grand Opening to be held the following Monday there in Birmingham. I realized it was asking a lot for a political nobody like myself to be a part of something as big politically as the Alabama State Headquarters Grand Opening, but I had long since gotten over any reservations about going where normal folks fear to tread. I had actually written the poem for the Inauguration of Bill Clinton, but I was willing to use it if it meant I would be able to speak out for the American worker during the campaign.

When I sat down across the desk from Jeff in his office there in Alabama State Clinton Headquarters, I told him I had a poem for the occasion and then read it for him and asked did he want me to

J. R. HAMMOND

read it for the Grand Opening. He said it was a great poem, but he had a better idea. Would I do the speech I had done in Jasper for the Grand Opening?

Now this I didn't expect. Being asked to do my speech at the State HQ Grand Opening by someone from Little Rock meant I was not doing things on my own anymore. It meant I was an official Clinton spokesman. This meant they couldn't come back later and say I was not one of them. So I told him this: "Yes, I'll do my speech, but after the election I want to have input and access to the administration. I'll do all I can for Governor Clinton, but I do not want to be forgotten. "Of course," he said. "We won't forget you after the election."

Famous last words. Anyway, I was set up to do the first major speech of my life. This was not like Jasper, as there were going to be cameras and media types and the press and a crowd of people, to boot. I made ready. I polished up on my delivery, added punch where it needed it, and started counting down the hours.

August 16, 1992. Alabama State Clinton HQ, and you are there:

There was a big crowd, and things were heating up. There was a group of politicians gathered to take part in the festivities and make their own speeches. I was scheduled to go on around 5 p.m. All of Alabama's Democratic congressmen were there, and the inimitable Senator Howell Heflin.

Finally, I was the next to go on. I walked up to the mike and looked out on all those faces looking back at me. They had gotten quiet.

I had polished up my delivery to the point that I wasn't nervous, just excited. I started out slowly, carefully, driving home the points about my role in the DNC and my involvement in the Clinton campaign. I was so pumped up that I read the first page of my two-page speech on short breaths, trying not to have a gap of silence. But I had to turn the page, and I inhaled at the same time.

I finished the line at the bottom of the first page and stopped talking, while I grabbed a breath and went to page two of my speech. I was looking down at the page, able to hear what was going on there in the crowd. There was total silence. Hundreds of people were not ten feet away, and you could have heard a pin drop. I looked up at the audience, and all eyes were on me. I launched into the rest of my speech, only this time after I made a point, I would stop and give the crowd a chance to cheer and applaud, which they did. As I was wrapping up, I made a mental note to leave spaces in my speech for the crowd reaction.

I finished, thanked them, and stepped down from the mike. I walked over to the side and stood by myself, watching the rest of the speakers. I was joined quickly by groups of one and two people who came over to shake my hand.

I knew the Huntsville/Madison County HQ was having its grand opening in two days, and I really enjoyed giving speeches, so I got myself invited to speak there, too. I dedicated myself to making the Huntsville speech one to remember. I would practice in front of a mirror, and I would give a speech that would stir souls.

It was a bright, pretty day in Huntsville. There was a bigger crowd than in Birmingham, probably 500 people. Governor Jim Folsom was there, and when he saw me he said "Hi, Working Man." That made me feel good.

When I went on, I spoke with a clarity and power that any politician would be proud of. Eight times during my speech I had to stop and allow the applause to die down. I had the good Huntsville Democrats eating out of my hand.

Governor Jim Folsom followed me, and his first words to the audience were these: "I guess there's nothing left to say. Working Man has said it all."

Everybody was super nice to me, and all in all, I thoroughly enjoyed it. I suppose you would think I would have made more speeches, since I was so good at it, but I made only one more—two months later—in Fayette, Alabama. There was a big crowd there, also.

In between my speeches, I had one more interview on the largest television station in Alabama, Birmingham's Channel 6 (WBRC-TV, ABC). It was a dandy. I led off the 10 p.m. news on September 3, 1992. The seven and one-half minute interview was aired four times, so I got Bill Clinton 30 minutes of free air time on Alabama's most watched station. This interview was so widely viewed that for a long while afterwards, total strangers would come up and want to shake my hand. One guy who was a Republican said he couldn't vote for Clinton, but he really admired what I had tried to do. The next poll that came out in mid-September had Bill Clinton in front of George Bush in Alabama for the first and only time during the campaign.

While I can't argue that my efforts alone were responsible for

*I met both Alabama Senators, Richard Shelby on the left, and Howell Heflin on the right, during the campaign.*

the support Clinton was getting, I did work very hard for the Democratic ticket in 1992 in Alabama. And it is interesting to look at the percentage breakdowns of the polls at that time. In south Alabama, where the Channel 6 signal will not reach, Bush beat Clinton soundly. In central Alabama, where some people can pick up Channel 6, it was a dead heat. But in the northern one-third of Alabama, where my 30 minutes of interviews were seen, Bill Clinton had a 10-point lead, enough to put him ahead for the only time in the race.

But the state Clinton organization had their own people in mind for the various speaking jobs in the campaign, and I didn't figure into their plans. I was out. After my 30-minute commercial for Bill Clinton, Albert Gore, and the Democratic Party in general had helped put Clinton in front for the only time during the campaign, I was no longer one of the team. I was told they wanted me to go on a bus tour of northern Alabama, but it went off without me. I was not a regular Party person, so in Alabama I was a nonperson.

This was very disappointing to me personally and politically. Personally, I enjoyed being involved with the campaign, and I had dedicated myself to improving my speaking and other political skills so that I could be even more involved. I think I had proved at that point that people liked my speeches and that the news media liked working with me. Politically, it was even more disappointing to be shoved aside in the campaign because this was just a continuation of the very problem I had been addressing since I qualified to run as a delegate: namely that the working man and woman was not allowed to be a part of the insider politics of the Democrats. And I knew this was bad for the Party and bad for the grassroots American and ultimately bad for the country.

So you can imagine how it made me feel when, on the one hand average people were coming up to me saying they liked what I said on TV or at a speech and were going to vote for Clinton, while on the other hand, the big wheels who ran the Party and the Clinton campaign quickly forgot my phone number.

I went to the election night party in Birmingham, and it was a festive occasion. I saw some of the people I had actually become friends with during the campaign (Jim Allbright, for one) and pretty much hung around watching all the goings-on. The campaign leadership went on stage and called out the names of those who had helped in the state of Alabama, and, even though they knew I was there, I was not mentioned. It doesn't matter now, but it was an insult to my face that night.

Bush carried Alabama, but Clinton was elected.

# 5

## Aftermath

# CHAPTER 22

## With Appreciation, Bill Clinton

Towards the end of November 1992, I received a phone call from my friend, Jim Allbright, President of the Alabama AFL-CIO. He had been to a labor function where he met an actual member of the Clinton transition team. He had told this guy about me and had his address. He suggested I send him a résumé.

So I had someone to write to on the inside. I had no real résumé per se, as I had never done anything but work in the coal mine. So I wrote a seven-page speech/résumé and sent it in to this member of the Clinton transition team. I told him all about myself, what I had done as the Voice of the American Worker at the DNC, and how I had come back to Alabama and been an official Clinton spokesman, speaking at Jasper, the Alabama state headquarters grand opening in Birmingham, the Huntsville grand opening, Birmingham again, Bessemer, and finally Fayette. I told him of the seven television interviews I had arranged, the 30 minutes of free air time I had received on September 3rd-4th that was viewed by an audience of an estimated one million Alabamians, and the nationwide interview that had been broadcast on PBS the night of September 25, which was a Friday night and was shown during prime time, and it had an audience of over 13 million. I told them in a nice way that it would be a crime against the working people of America if the one rank-and-file laborer to play an actual nationwide role in the election of President Clinton was left out, and that I deserved to be the Voice of the American Worker within the White House. It was a forceful document, full of grassroots rhetoric and blazing with the vision of one seeking simple justice for the American worker. I also included letters of recommendation from the state president of the Alabama AFL-CIO and from my friend, Alabama Secretary of State Billy Joe

Camp. I made a passionate plea for making the working class a partner in how things were going to run in this country.

It was a good résumé, especially considering I was just a coal miner. I mailed it to the address Jim had given me and tried not to be impatient.

I got my reply on Christmas Eve. Around 11 a.m, the phone rang and when I answered, it was a member of the Clinton Transition Team calling, the one to whom I had sent the résumé.

"Hello," he said, "is this the Working Man? I'm with the transition team and I got the résumé you sent. May I say first, Working Man, what an eloquent writer you are. It was a real pleasure to read through the information you sent. I just wanted to tell you how impressed with you we are. Bill Clinton needs a man like you. No, that's not right. Bill Clinton doesn't need a man like you. Bill Clinton needs you. All I work with is personnel, and I can assure you that you are going to be in demand. Well, I'll be in touch, so be ready. Good-bye, Working Man."

Well, was this a fine Christmas present or what?

Sadly, I never heard another word from him or anyone else in the Transition Team. As Inauguration Day grew near, and I couldn't get hold of anybody that had ever heard of the Working Man, a sense of real depression fell across me.

Sixteen months earlier, in August of '92, I had been asked twice by my Clinton delegate coordinator, Mr. Glen Rushing, if I would be able to get off work for union business to work for the Clinton campaign. The former president of my Local, now president of UMWA District 20, Mr. John Stewart, a great American Leader, was going to see to getting me the necessary off time when the call came. It never did. Then a member of the Clinton transition team called me on Christmas Eve Day to tell me I was the man for the job as a liaison between the administration and the American worker.

Nonetheless, I was still 1,300 feet deep in the coal mine, with evidently zero access to the White House. As January 20th drew closer, and the details began to come about the Inaugural events, I saw the handwriting on the wall. I was officially once again a nonperson in the Democratic Party.

To top it off, 116 people from across the country were flown to Washington, D.C., with their room and board and even new clothes paid for by corporate America. These were people Clinton and/or Mrs. Rodham-Clinton had met during the campaign and invited up there for the Inauguration. Had they done more than I had for the Clinton campaign? Yet I was on the outside looking in.

Remember I told you Irene the mule got even with me for upstaging her at the Democratic National Convention? Well, she was the Alabama entrant in the Inaugural parade, while I—the Voice of the American Worker—stayed home.

I thought this was another symbol of the public relations problems political parties have with middle-class America. The party powers-that-be are so caught up in themselves that they fail to hear what is being said by Joe Citizen. In fact, there was a press release by the Alabama Democratic Party leadership late in '93 to the effect that they had identified problem areas and had hired a consultant firm to help them change their image. It seems to me, if you have a poor Party image, work on the Party, not the image. But I'm just a coal miner. What do I know?

∽

With the Inauguration over, and Governor Bill Clinton now officially President Bill Clinton, I decided to try a more direct approach and actually contacted the White House. Since the guy from the transition team had told me he dealt with personnel, I decided to call the White House Personnel Office.

This was my first adventure with the executive branch.

I called the White House switchboard and got the White House Personnel Office. I explained how I was the Voice of the American Worker at the DNC, how I gave speeches for President Clinton, including one at the Alabama State Headquarters, and how I arranged many interviews, and worked hard as a grass-roots American for Clinton's election. Now I wanted to help run the country. The staff member told me how impressive I sounded and to send a résumé immediately. This person was very friendly. I sent a résumé, photos of myself on stage at the DNC, and a chat letter. I called back later, and I was told the person I had been dealing with was gone and was beyond reach. So I got their phone number from information and called their home. It was not a good move, as this made this person angry at me. My White House connection was broken.

Then, there was a story in the *Birmingham News* about two Alabama women in positions of power in the White House: Joan Bagget, Director of the Office of Political Affairs, and Alexis Herman, Director of the White House Office of Public Liaison.

I called both of their offices and explained to the staff members that answered about my role in the Clinton election. Being able to say I was a delegate to the DNC helped. I was rewarded for my efforts on April 6, 1993, when I got a phone call from Joan Baggett herself. It was a very pleasant chat, and I told her I wanted to help run the country. She told me to send her a résumé, and of course I did. I got a letter from her later, telling me I was more valuable at home. I also got nowhere with the Office of the Public Liaison, except to be asked to send a résumé. I did enjoy working with the person from the Office of the Public Liaison. Thanks to you from the Working Man.

So, it was repeatedly thanks but no thanks. It was hard to swallow, being told you were part of things but not really being so. But what was really lost was the chance to give grass-roots, blue-collar American workers some input where it could really make a difference.

I tried to deal with the White House in a straightforward manner, telling them what I had done and that I wanted to help run the country. Every one of the people I dealt with in the White House was very cordial, and for that I thank them. But if you are an average person and you try to deal with the White House, be prepared not to get a lot done. It can be very trying.

⌁

So now I am just a coal miner again, albeit one with an interesting story. An average guy that every day on the news sees someone he knows personally, be it local, state, or national coverage. I've seen the Jewish guy, Rhom Shapiro, on television several times; he is one of the leaders of the national Democratic Party and the guy who gave me the invitation to the party at the top of the Chrysler Building. And the people I dealt with in the White House show up on the news from time to time.

I also got a Christmas card from Bill and Hilary, and Albert and Tipper, too. I have them all put together in a big frame as sort of a collage of political involvement. It's eye catching, to say the least. I carried the White House Christmas card around and let strangers look at it. I figured ordinary people might have wanted to see what a card from the President looks like. Everybody I showed it to seemed to enjoy it.

I borrowed the title of this chapter from the photo President

Clinton sent me, signed "With Appreciation, Bill Clinton." It somehow seemed to fit so well. There are those that now say I was lucky just to get a photo, and that I must have been one totally naive individual to have believed the things I was being told by the Clinton campaign and the Clinton White House.

Well, maybe I am naive. I know I am guilty of believing that the government ought to be run for the benefit of the great mass of people who make it all possible, the working men and women of America. And I am guilty of believing that the Clinton campaign offered hope of correcting some of the indifference to working people's issues that had been building up during the previous 12 years of Republican policies. And I am guilty of believing that the people who are best qualified to speak about the issues of working people are the working people themselves. In other words, someone just like me.

# CHAPTER 23

## The Final Chapter

In my sojourn from the depths of the coal mines to the heights of my face-to-face meeting with soon-to-be President Clinton there on the stage at Madison Square Garden on the closing night of the 1992 Democratic National Convention, I pushed forward with only one thought in mind: I would do all I could to gain access to the Clinton administration for the American working class. I would deal with the people who run the country in a manner befitting those tens of millions of people for whom I was the only true representative operating in the circles in which I found myself. I am one of the few average, rank-and-file, blue collar, American workers ever elected a delegate to the Democratic National Convention.

Because I was not actually a regular within the Democratic Party, I had no obligations to anyone except other blue-collar Americans—not to the Democratic Party, not to anyone in the Democratic Party. But this also meant that no one in the Party was obligated to me.

And this is one of the things that is wrong with the American political process and which makes it so hard for average people to be involved and to bring about changes that are needed.

This is why in the end I was lied to, used, and ultimately left out of the Clinton administration. Those same people who told me repeatedly that I was part of things during the DNC, that I was part of things during the Campaign, and that I would be a part of and have access to the new administration—those people are now running the country, and they don't want someone like me around. Being around the Ivy League suit-boys was a learning experience.

∽

But people, I sure had an adventure. I promise you I'm not trying to brag, but it was at points unreal.

The media and regular political types ridiculed me when I ran for delegate under the name Working Man, but I was able to rub their noses in it when I won.

Ross Perot, a man who will go down in the history books, had a direct bearing on my life by spending $16 million of his own money telling folks to vote Uncommitted, which let me be elected a delegate to the 1992 Democratic National Convention.

The movie star, Mary Steenburgen, sat next to me on the bus, and a U.S. Congressman bought me lunch.

I elected myself Mayor of Woodstock, Alabama, a city that in fact does not exist, so that I could wine and dine for free in the hospitality suite with actual elected Democratic officials, one of whom I had drinks and talked football with and who turned out to be the Lieutenant Governor of South Carolina.

I was made an honorary citizen of the great state of North Carolina, and I took a moonlight stroll down New York's Lexington Avenue with a true Southern belle of the first magnitude.

I will never forget being told, "Governor Clinton knows how hard you've worked this week, Working Man, but he has one more job for you; He wants you to join him on stage tonight after his acceptance speech to meet him and represent the working people of America."

I was on television eleven times, three times nationwide, and was an actual spokesman for the man who is now President.

I made speeches all over Alabama, at the request of the Clinton campaign, and total strangers came up to me and told me they were glad to know me and liked what I had to say.

I have my own personalized autographed photo of the President, and was on the White House Christmas card list for one year, anyway.

It was the time of my life, in many ways.

But of all the things I did, the one thing I feel the deepest about, the one thing that is most satisfying to my soul, is that I really did try to do something for all of working-class America. I wish I could have done more. I hoped to get continuing input and access to the White House so that we working types wouldn't be getting the shaft all the time, and not be the caboose of this American train by being the last in line anytime something comes up.

I didn't. I'm genuinely sorry, people. We for sure needed it, because President Clinton has so far done a lot that rubs working people the wrong way. When I look back at the speeches I made, and the things I said Bill Clinton would do for working people and the nation in general, I have to admit to my fellow workers that this administration has floundered in many areas.

The middle-class tax cut that Governor Clinton promised looks to us as if it has turned into a President Clinton tax increase. Despite all the rhetoric, it seems we are no closer to health care reform than we were during the campaign.

The much-publicized $200 haircut, the gays in the military issue, NAFTA, and Whitewater make working people wonder where the President is getting his advice.

It makes us feel that the Ivy League suit-boys have taken control, and we know they have no experience at working for a living and no concept of what makes this nation tick. They have never gone without health insurance.

If I—or some other working person—had been in a position to give you advice, I could have told you that homosexual rights are not a burning issue and that making this your first big issue to push was politically wrong. Hey, I don't care who anyone sleeps with as long as it doesn't interfere with my life or cost me money. But from the start you put your adminstration in the doghouse with every American veteran. Of course you weren't in the military. I wasn't, either. But I know who has kept this country free through the years.

Since I didn't get the opportunity to speak up within the Clinton administration about the issues facing America today, I want to close with a few things that I hear working people express concerns about. Mr. President, I respectfully suggest that you take notes.

The reason you were elected was because you promised America a tax cut for the middle class. Every pay day, working people in this country look at their paychecks and curse. We are taxed to death, Mr. President.

We have got to get a grip on the federal entitlements or all is lost.

Everybody in this country able to work should work—men, women, and especially mothers on welfare. If they are busy working and raising a family, I guarantee you they will not want any more kids.

One thing working black people and working white people agree on is that we don't like people too sorry to work.

Men who father children and then won't support them should be prosecuted and punished.

On health care, we first need to take care of the 37 million workers who have no coverage. Building a national health care system will take time, but we've got to take the first step. The burden ought to be on the employers. In the coal mines, for example, the companies benefit every time we pick up a shovel. It is their responsibility as part of the capitalistic system to pay for medical care. But start with those who have no coverage.

If your house is in disorder, clean it up. Don't get mad because other people say you have a problem.

⏝

To the citizens, I have one more modest proposal to put forth. I have a way to make this great and beautiful nation work on a political level. This is a way to make the special interests get in the back seat while we the people drive for a while. It's a way to make this country work for those who actually go to work. This is a plan for those who pay their taxes and raise their children in a supportive and loving manner so that they have the best chance of being good American citizens, so that they, too, will raise their children to become good, productive, American, working-class citizens.

Working-class America, listen up. I am now going to tell you how we the people, as mentioned in the Constitution, can take this country away from those who have, for too long, run it as a personal checking account, take it away from those who have tried to use it as an ongoing experiment in Sociology 101, take it away from those concerned with issues that grass roots America does not care about.

Here is the problem: There are no working-class people in the U.S. Congress, and no working-class governors. There are some who may have at one time been regular guys, but politics has a way of cutting those involved off from the electorate. I didn't meet one ordinary person, other than myself, at the Democratic National Committee, and there are not any ordinary people running this country now.

It takes money, millions of dollars, to run for office. The rich and powerful have the money it takes to run, and they aren't talking to us. Working types like myself are too busy to go out and raise the money it takes to run. If one of us were to run against a big name politician, we would lose. But in that last sentence lies the key to working-class America getting our country back.

The key word was "One." There are a few rich and powerful with millions. There are millions of us with a few dollars.

So we run for office.

Hundreds of us. Thousands of us. We run for office. We must have brave men and women—citizens not in politics in any way, not connected or beholden—to scrape up the money somehow and put their name on the ballot and run for office.

The power of incumbency is name recognition. They have the millions of dollars. We, on the other hand, have millions of warm bodies with names that could go on the ballots, enough names to confuse the issue. Normally, there are a few names on the ballot for the really important offices. Let's put 50 on the ballot. Let's put 100 on the ballot. If enough of us run for Congress from each Congressional district, the incumbent's name will get lost in the shuffle somewhere, and some of us will win by accident—just like I did in 1992.

Instead of buying a new big screen television, run for Congress. It is our only chance. For unless we get some people who are not professional politicians in that U.S. Congress, all will be lost. The best thing is that once just one of us has made it, the facade that has become the political norm will be shattered forever.

I have seen firsthand how arrogant and deceitful politics is, how honor is nonexistent, how back-stabbing people once you don't need them is a common practice. We can run the government just as well as these Ivy League lawyers, once we get a little on the job training. With the government in the shape it's in, anything is worth a try if it will give grass-roots America its say-so in running things. So, we must become involved.

↬

To my bosses, I want to say I have worked for the Jim Walter Corporation for 20 years at the #3 coal mine in Jefferson County, Alabama. I plan to go to Tampa, Florida, on a book-signing trip when I can. So if anybody in the CMO there in Tampa wants to know how to make the Mining Division work better and make more money, I'll be glad to come by and tell you which of your management personnel needs their tail fired. No extra charge.

↬

To the Democratic Party, let me say this: you people missed a great opportunity. Nothing would have shown you to be a part of the working class better than having an ordinary guy be able to rise up from nowhere and participate with you.

↜

To my readers, I really hope you liked this book. It took me over a year to write it, and it was a minor miracle it got published. Thanks to you all, and may God bless you and yours. Don't live with your head in the sand, and don't be afraid to make the effort.

And I hope Tom Selleck plays me in the movie.

↜

Well, I guess that just about wraps it up. I lived a real true-life adventure. I hope you have some adventure in your life, too. Take care of your families, and have patience with your children and your loved ones. Be nice to each other. Teach your children to fight for what's right, in their spare time off the job.

*And a free bonus for Crimson Tide Fans . . .*

## THE BEST OF THE NATION
## WEARS CRIMSON AND WHITE

By J. R. "Working Man" Hammond

You can ask anybody you happen to meet,
Anywhere in the country and on any street,

Which team sparkles like a beacon, in the blackness of night.
The best of the Nation wears Crimson and White.

If you're looking for symbols of courage today,
And for those that uphold the American way,

In the heart of Dixie one fact shines so bright.
The best of the Nation wears Crimson and White.

Like the Heart of darkness will hide from the sun,
Men of valor will fight 'til the battle is won.

And uphold the honor of past generations,
And prove they're the best in this greatest of Nations.

For here in the deep South we cherish the truth,
And all do our best to instill in our youth,

The spirit of Justice, and of doing what's right.
The best of the Nation wears Crimson and White.

And though it's just a game, it's so much like life.
As we each battle turmoil and trouble and strife.

Here in Alabama, we all stand and salute with pride,
Coach Stallings, his family
And the University of Alabama,
The Mighty Crimson Tide.

*And a final, final word in honor of our military . . .*

TO THOSE WHO SERVED
(Memorial Day, 1994)

By J. R. "Working Man" Hammond


We owe so much to those who served.
And fought,
And died.

For without your courage
We would not be here.

Let freedom ring
Would be forgotten.

And the world would be a barren place,
Where the forces of evil
Drain away the lives of the innocent.

This nation was forged in the heat of rifle ~~life,~~ FIRE,
And hammered out on the anvil of war
By blacksmiths of liberty,
Millworkers in the foundry of Democracy.

As surely as God went with those who served,
He has opened Heaven's gates to our fallen,
And they rest with him.